KEITH
ROWLEY'S
WOODTURNING PROJECTS

KEITH ROWLEY'S
WOODTURNING PROJECTS

GUILD OF MASTER CRAFTSMAN PUBLICATIONS LTD

First published 1996 by
Guild of Master Craftsman Publications Ltd,
166 High Street, Lewes,
East Sussex BN7 1XU

© Keith Rowley 1996

ISBN 1 86108 013 1

Black-and-white photography by Geoff Ford
(except, see below)
Black-and-white photography by Pete Walton, pages 13
(left), 17, 18 (left), 24 (bottom), 25, 29 (bottom), 30, 35,
36, 41 (bottom), 42, 46 (bottom), 47, 56, 57, 65, 66, 75,
76, 85 (bottom), 86, 93 (right), 94, 99 (right), 100, 107
(bottom), 108 (left), 114 (bottom), 115, 122 (bottom),
130 (bottom), 131, 139 (bottom), 140, 148 (bottom), 159

Colour photography by Pete Walton

Illustrations by Geoff Ford

Designed by Ian Hunt

Typeface: Berkeley

Printed and bound by Thanet Press, Margate, England

DEDICATION

This book is dedicated to the memory of my late father, who taught me to appreciate the beauty of trees and wood, and persuaded me to follow a trade working with them, and to my mother for instilling in me the need to respect nature and creation.

Also to my wife Jean, who has always provided unfailing support and encouragement in both the professions I have followed, and lastly to my son, daughter and five grandchildren, with the hope that one or more of them might follow in grandad's footsteps.

ACKNOWLEDGEMENTS

My heartfelt thanks are extended to the editorial staff at GMC Publications and in particular to Commissioning Editor Elizabeth Inman.

In addition to always being there to lean on for advice and assistance, she has always been extremely patient and kind to me.

I am again greatly indebted to Geoff Ford who has spent many hours in my workshop preparing the sequence photographs and drawings, which are of the same high standard I have come to expect from him.

To my good friend, David Francis, I extend many thanks for all the assistance he has given me and in particular for the making of the brass fitting on the finger-ring stand.

I also extend my thanks to Alan and Stuart Batty, Mike Cripps, Tony Bunce, Jim Gilbert and Len Smith for their assistance with certain aspects of this book; and to Robert Sorby Ltd; Craft Supplies Ltd and Axminster Power Tool Company, all having cooperated fully with equipment use and advice.

Finally, I offer a special thanks to three outstanding professional woodturners who I feel privileged to call friends, namely Ray Key, Bert Marsh and Chris Stott.

All three have graced my workshop from time to time and willingly passed on advice and assistance with all matters connected with turning wood.

AUTHOR'S NOTE

The popularity of woodturning continues on an upward curve. The availability of more leisure time, either enforced through redundancy or by choice through early retirement, is a contributory factor but, in my view, is not the most important reason.

I believe that the greatest single reason for the ever-growing popularity of crafts like woodturning is because more and more people are beginning to realize that satisfaction through creative work is an essential requirement of our nature. Unless we make room in our lives for it, we may well live under the shadow of a sense of futility and frustration.

In the woodwork room of the school I attended, there hung a slice of oak board on which were carved the words, 'None so forlorn as the craftless man'. I do not know to whom these words should be credited, but I do know that they convey a most important message, and that they have had a profound effect on me since my schooldays.

'Whatsoever thy hand findeth to do, do it with thy might' (Ecclesiastes 9:10).

MEASUREMENTS

Although care has been taken to ensure that metric measurements are true and accurate, they are only conversions from imperial. Throughout the book instances will be found where an imperial measurement has slightly varying metric equivalents, usually within 0.5mm either way, because in each particular case the closest metric equivalent has been given. Care should be taken to use *either* imperial *or* metric measurements consistently throughout a project. (*See* also Metric Conversion Table, page 164.)

PROJECTS

At the start of each project, an estimated time is given, within which the work can be completed. This is meant as a guide only, as different people work at different speeds.

Each project has also been given a difficulty rating, which appears alongside the time guide. One star indicates the simplest projects, five stars the most complex.

Contents

Foreword

Some twelve years ago, Keith Rowley and I were both embarking upon early retirement. He had returned to his first love, woodturning, and I was just beginning to battle with its mysteries. We first met at a national woodworking exhibition, where Keith was demonstrating a Coronet Major lathe. As I had acquired an earlier model, I quickly joined his audience.

His consummate skills and relaxed approach with the crowds, to whom he offered much invaluable advice in an easy manner, immediately attracted me. On discovering that Keith offered two-day courses for the likes of me, I signed up without further ado.

Keith caught me in the nick of time, before too many bad habits were acquired. On returning home to the first session in the workshop, shavings were flying everywhere with the greatest of ease and bowl after bowl emerged effortlessly.

This anecdote not only demonstrates that Keith had mastered the skills of turning long, long ago, but also, and just as importantly, that he possesses the ability to impart those skills to others. In the intervening years, he has become a well known and popular demonstrator at woodworking shows and exhibitions countrywide, as well as at international woodworking seminars.

Like many others, my immediate desire was to produce bowls, ignoring Keith's philosophy that the mastery of spindle-turning skills ensures an equally capable and successful headstock turner. With hindsight, he was right, and although spindle turning attracted me less at the outset, thanks to Keith, I am now equally at home with either approach.

His belief in the importance of mastering spindle-turning skills is apparent in both this and his earlier book, *Woodturning: A Foundation Course*. When family, friends and odd acquaintances have become sated with 'desirable gifts', turners are often left wondering, 'What next?'. Keith supplies the answer, offering a range of projects that have proved 'great little money spinners'. And as well as financing necessary materials, and perhaps a few extra items of equipment, bouts of repetition turning really do work marvels in enhancing the skills. A wise old bird is Keith.

Years ago, if someone had asked me to produce a batch of fifty identical garden dibbers or aromatic bowls, I would have been petrified. No longer is this the case, and now I positively welcome the telephone call, 'Could you . . . ?'. I regularly supply the garden shop of one of Britain's stately homes, and thoroughly enjoy those shavings flying as I produce my batches – all identical, well finished and obviously a pleasure to handle. Thank you, Keith.

The many who appreciated Keith's first volume will undoubtedly now be ready to further hone their skills and design sense, and with the help of these pages, quickly progress from the humdrum to dizzier heights. There are twenty classic projects to follow, all graded for difficulty, with a suggested making time. Now it's up to you – and may your pieces become classics too!

John Haywood
Stoke Abbott, Dorset
1996

Chapter 1
Introduction

The main objective of this book is to provide ideas and guidelines for making a range of projects to suit most levels of proficiency, from simple craft fair items to quite difficult projects. It is the result of the many comments and remarks made to me at the demonstrations I give nationally and locally. Apparently there are many turners who, having acquired a certain level of technical skill, are searching for new ideas for things to make, and methods of making them.

This is *not* a book about the techniques of woodturning, and is not intended as a book for *complete* beginners. My first book, *Woodturning: A Foundation Course*, was aimed at the beginner, and describes in detail the techniques of cutting wood, tool sharpening, safety, and so on. I suggest that anyone who needs an introduction to the basics of the craft should refer to *Woodturning: A Foundation Course* before embarking on the projects contained in this book. *This is particularly important from the point of view of safety*. I have chosen to deal with specific safety aspects as they occur, although the basic safety rules are also included on page 160.

Where appropriate, reminders of some fundamental techniques are mentioned, as I believe that we all learn not only from practice but also from constant reiteration. Where and when alternative or advanced techniques can be advantageously applied, I discuss and fully describe them.

The expense of setting up in woodturning can be quite considerable, particularly if the aspiring turner buys a lathe from the top end of the range. Even the purchase of a modestly priced lathe can be expensive when added to the cost of a basic set of tools and a grinder.

Many turners, in order to recover some of this outlay quickly, prefer to concentrate on making fairly simple objects – proven good sellers – for which further expenditure in the form of timber is kept to a minimum. Starting with these easier projects also allows the development of skill and technique, as well as confidence and feel.

The best way to improve technique and speed is to do repetition work on simple projects, such as the quickest projects in the early part of this book. If you are a beginner, I suggest that you produce at least 50 light pulls, toadstools, eggs, or whatever else you fancy, before you pass on to the more difficult projects. This way you are likely to be rewarded not only financially, but also by increased confidence and skill!

Although each project has a paragraph headed 'Design Considerations', this book does not deal specifically with the subject of design, as many books and articles on design are readily available.

Some turners believe that a structured approach to design and observance of the 'golden rules' are essential. Others, myself included, prefer the 'intuitive' approach to design, based on the development of a 'good eye', through observation and critical assessment of one's own work and that of other turners, and of course artefacts in porcelain, glass, silver, and so on.

The 20 projects I have described have not, to the best of my knowledge, been previously published, although I am unable to guarantee that this is the case. If I have inadvertently included ideas that others believe to be originally theirs, I can only say that this is completely unintentional and apologize unreservedly.

I have sought to provide a balance between the amount of headstock and spindle turning included in the book. My personal view is that many turners concentrate too much on headstock turning (bowl turning in particular) without having developed their spindle-turning skills.

To be a really good headstock turner, you must first have thoroughly mastered the technique of *cutting* wood needed in spindle turning, where all shortcomings in technique and discipline are quickly exposed.

In many of the projects, I have placed great emphasis on making and using home-made jigs and templates, not only as a means of speeding up production, but also to give greater accuracy in setting out, sawing and boring, and the like.

It is fair to say that some of the projects included in this book are more easily made when ancillary machines and equipment are available. Consequently, I have included the chapter 'Ancillary Equipment', in which I offer advice not only on the purchase of such equipment as the bandsaw, pillar drill, router, and so on, but also on safe methods of use. I must stress, however, that, when I mention particular makes of machines or tools, they are merely those that I use and which reflect my personal preferences. You will find many other machines and tools on the market which will serve you equally well.

The projects are presented in what I consider to be ascending order of difficulty, and each has been allocated a 'difficulty rating', with one star indicating the easiest projects and five stars the most complex. Additionally, I have given the estimated time required to produce each project, based on average ability. It must be appreciated that what may be considered easy by some may well be considered difficult by others, and vice versa. 'Average ability' is impossible to define precisely, so readers must be prepared to use their own judgement as well as the guidelines.

I do not for a moment claim that all the designs, tips and hints contained in this book have been conceived in my own head. I have always tried to observe and learn from the work of other turners and to listen carefully to their views and methods. It is inevitable, therefore, that some of the ideas and 'wrinkles' mentioned may well have been picked up from other turners. Some may have been modified and, dare I say, improved to suit my own style or work in hand. Let me, however, dispel any idea that only turners of long experience or established reputation have the monopoly on good ideas and design. Complete beginners have also been a source of inspiration to me.

The design of each project is offered as an example only and is not intended to be definitive. I shall feel very flattered if you wish to copy any or all of the projects, but would encourage you to modify or improve them to suit your own particular purpose and liking.

Suggested finishing methods for each project are included, but this topic has also been the subject of complete books, so the type of finish is left very much to individual preference.

Finally, I have set out to present the book in an 'easy to read' style. I therefore trust that everyone who reads this book will find something to engage their interest, and persuade them to have a go.

Here's wishing you many happy hours of woodturning!

Chapter 2
Ancillary Equipment

As the woodturning bug bites deeper and the shock of the initial outlay for the necessities (lathe, turning tools and grinder) subsides, many turners will want to consider the acquisition of other items of equipment.

In my first book, *Woodturning: A Foundation Course*, I suggested that until a fair degree of experience had been obtained, it was not advisable to start splashing out on ancillary equipment and expensive chucks.

This advice still holds good, but there comes the time when extra equipment makes the turner's life much more comfortable, speeds up production and removes the drudgery of preparing such things as bowl blanks by using hand tools. (Buying bowl blanks already cut is much more expensive than buying through and through boards and cutting your own discs.)

I possess a fair amount of ancillary equipment, including a planer, circular saw, spindle moulder, mortiser, bandsaws, belt and disc sander, routers, power drill and screwdriver, pillar drill with a whole variety of boring bits, and several expensive chucking systems and lathe steadies.

I am not suggesting you need anything like this array of equipment, but it makes my life as a professional turner (and sometimes cabinet-maker), much easier. In order of priority, I feel that consideration should be given by the serious woodturner to buying a bandsaw, a reliable and versatile chucking system, a pillar drill and boring bits, a lightweight router, and perhaps a steady. To make all the projects that follow in this book, most of these are required if drudgery, frustration and irritation are to be avoided.

I therefore propose to offer advice on the choice and use of such equipment, with particular emphasis on safety.

BANDSAWS

Next to the lathe and bench grinder, the bandsaw is the most used item of equipment in my everyday production work. It is extremely versatile and safe and easy to operate as long as you use your common sense. A continuous band of cutting edge where the thrust is downward makes it much safer than the circular saw. This arrangement has several other advantages, one being that it allows a more gentle and far deeper cut than the circular saw with a much smaller electric motor. Another advantage is that the narrow kerf of the saw blade results in much less waste, an important consideration when resawing expensive wood. Finally, the cost of a bandsaw blade is only a fraction of the cost of a good circular saw blade.

The cost of a new bandsaw varies considerably according to its suitability (and quality) for heavy, medium or light duty. The 'Startrite' model 352 shown in Fig 2.1 is my heavy-duty floor-standing bandsaw and, being of excellent quality, it will cost well in excess of £1,000 to buy new.

For lighter duty application, and for demonstration purposes, I also own a much smaller bench-type bandsaw, the 'Tyme' BS20 model (*see* Fig 2.2). This is easily transportable and would probably satisfy the needs of most woodturners. The cost of this is very modest indeed.

Both have tables that tilt to 45° (an important consideration when wishing to convert square stock to octagon before heavy-duty turning), and both come with rip and mitre guides. While acknowledged as being one of the safest machines in the woodworking field, it is important that the manufacturer's instructions on setting up, maintenance and operation are strictly complied with.

Some of the most important considerations in the interests of safety and quality of operation are to choose the correct width of blade for the job in hand and to make sure that it is sharp and correctly set. Ripping is best

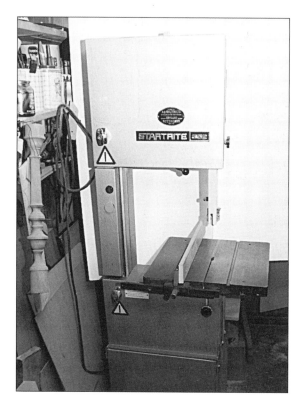

Fig 2.1 The 'Startrite' 352 floor-standing bandsaw –
a very robust and efficient machine.

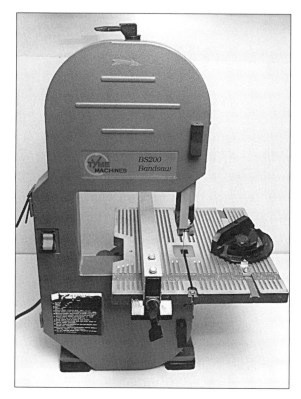

Fig 2.2 The 'Tyme' BS200 bench-mounted bandsaw
which is ideal for the small workshop.

achieved with as wide a blade as possible, and
the feed rate should be slow and smooth. A
push stick should always be used, and you
must keep your fingers well away from the
blade. Eye protection is also an absolute must.

When cutting discs, it is vital that the
correct width of blade is used. It is impossible
to be precise on the smallest radius any given
size of blade will cut, as much will depend on
the species of wood and the skill of the
operator. Most handbooks provide a chart
offering a basic guide on this point.

I strongly recommend that you do further
and more detailed reading on bandsaw practice.
There are many good books available to buy or
borrow from the library.

My final advice on the buying of a bandsaw
is to visit one of the many woodworking
exhibitions that are held. Not only is it possible
to get a very good deal (exhibitors do not like
carting heavy machines back), but also most of
the demonstrators are extremely competent and
well able to give you sound advice on the
machine best suited to your requirements.

CHUCKING SYSTEMS

There is an enormous variety of chucking
systems available to the woodturner, and I can
only comment on the systems I possess or have
tried when demonstrating.

A question very often posed to me at
demonstrations and the like is, 'What's the best
chuck I can buy?' My response is fairly
consistent. First, I enquire on what brand and
model of lathe it is intended to use it. For
example, it would be ridiculous of me to
recommend one of the largest and heaviest
chucks for a cheap lathe with small bearings
and headstock, as it would probably ruin the
lathe in no time.

Then I enquire what type of turning they
generally undertake and how much money they
are prepared to spend, and then offer my advice
accordingly.

My own lathes are made to cope with
medium- to heavy-duty work, and I prefer the
Axminster four-jaw chuck for many
applications (*see* Fig 2.3). It is expensive,
however, and the chuck, combined with the

Fig 2.3 The Axminster four-jaw chuck and some accessories are shown on the left and the Craft Supplies Precision Combination Chuck and accessories are shown on the right.

many accessories available for it, will set you back more than the price of many a lathe. It is extremely robust, accurate, quick and easy to use. For the professional turner it represents good value for money, and I commend it to anyone possessing a sturdy enough lathe to carry it. For Axminster Power Tool Company, *see* page 162.

Fig 2.4 The Craft Supplies Maxi-Grip 2000 chuck with its many accessories.

For years now I have also used the Craft Supplies Precision Combination Chuck, and also more recently their fairly new model, the Maxi-Grip 2000 (*see* Fig 2.4). Both chucks are precision made and easy to use, and the numerous accessories readily available for both models make them most versatile. Not being as heavy as the four-jaw chuck, they are suitable for most types of lathes and, of course, they are also much less expensive.

There are many other quality chucks on the market, and depending on the type of turning you intend to do, and the depth of your pocket, you will certainly find something that suits your needs.

It is a good idea to read the product reviews and advertisements in the woodworking magazines, and visit one of the major woodworking shows, so that you are fully informed of the range available. You will be spoilt for choice on chucking systems, so shop around, and buy the best you can afford that meets your requirements.

PILLAR DRILLS

Accurate drilling is extremely difficult with hand-held tools, and the drill press or pillar drill not only does this, but also provides the means to hold the workpiece firmly. The essential features are: the motor and a belt and range of pulleys that allow for a wide speed range; the chuck that holds the boring bits; the table, which is adjustable up and down (and sometimes tilting), and depth stops.

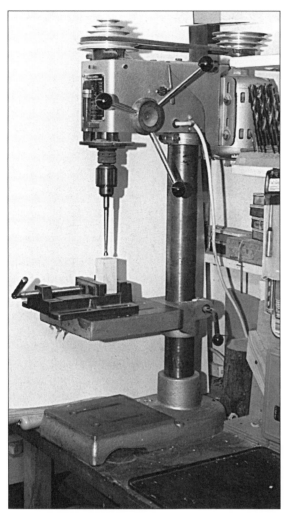

Fig 2.5 The 'Startrite' Mercury bench-mounted pillar drill. Note that the pulley and chuck guards have been removed for the purpose of the photograph only.

The bench-type pillar drill that I use is the 'Startrite' Mercury (*see* Fig 2.5), which is an engineering-quality machine and quite expensive. (Please note that the belt and chuck guards have been removed for the photograph. These must always be fitted when the machine is in use.)

Fortunately for the prospective buyer, the prices of many models are very competitive and, although not of engineering quality, some are more than adequate for woodworking operations.

BORING BITS

Many types of boring bits are available, and Fig 2.6 shows a variety of bits in everyday use in my own workshop.

Twist drills Those shown in the metal case on the photograph are essentially intended for metal drilling, but I use them a lot for drilling pilot holes, screw holes and countersinking.

Brad point drills These are the smallest drills in the wooden holder. The brad point provides for very accurate location and prevents 'skating'. They are also fairly accurate when drilling end grain.

Sawtooth cutters The largest bits in the wooden holder are sawtooth cutters. These are without doubt the best wood-boring bits

Fig 2.6 An assortment of drill bits used in my workshop – twist drills, brad point drills, sawtooth cutters and flat bits.

available but also the most expensive. They are ideal for quick, clean boring, and are also excellent for angle boring.

Flat bits The two bits lying flat on the bench. These are comparatively inexpensive and intended for high-speed application. They also perform fairly well in end grain.

Other types of bits are also available, but those shown serve my every need.

PILLAR DRILL JIGS AND ACCESSORIES

It is dangerous to rely on hand grip only when drilling on the machine. A drill press vice, shown gripping a short section of wood in Fig 2.5, is absolutely essential.

The number of jigs that can be made for the pillar drill are limited only by one's own imagination. Quite a few of the projects in this book require the use of such jigs, and they are fully described in the appropriate place.

PILLAR DRILL – SAFETY CONSIDERATIONS

- Always make sure the work is securely held.
- Guards must always be fitted and correctly positioned.
- Avoid loose, dangling sleeves – they can get caught up in the drill.
- Always wear eye protection.

- Choose the correct speed compatible with the size of bit to be used. The general rule is that the larger the drill bit, the lower the machine speed.
- Isolate the electrics when slipping the pulley belt to change speed.
- Read the manufacturer's operating instructions and observe them.

ROUTERS

The portable hand router is indispensable in joinery and cabinet-making shops. Its versatility extends to producing clean-cut rebates, mouldings, housings, and joints such as dovetails and mortise and tenons. Used with templates and jigs it will cut out repeated shapes and decorative grillwork.

It also has many useful applications for the woodturner and, in conjunction with home-made jigs fixed to the lathe, it can be used for fluting, reeding, slot mortising for tripod legs, and so on. Some of the projects I use it for are fluting turned columns associated with Adam fireplace surrounds, fluting component parts of standard lamps, applying reeding to four-poster bed components and for dowelling, slot mortising and dovetailing tripod legs to table columns.

For most woodturners, a light-duty router such as the one shown in Fig 2.7 is more than adequate and they are not terribly expensive. This router, in conjunction with the metal

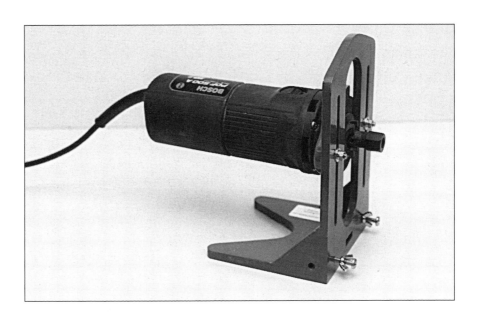

Fig 2.7 Bosch light-duty router and the 'Technic' carrier, used in many woodturning projects.

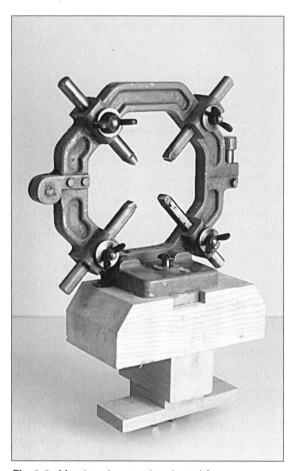

Fig 2.8 Metalturning steady, adapted for use on my woodturning lathe and invaluable for long, slender turnings.

carrier supporting it in the photograph, will be used in making the novelty clock (*see* page 66).

Safety in use of the router is basically the application of common sense, but it is still advisable to study the manufacturer's operating instructions and comply with them. Needless to say, *eye protection is essential.*

STEADY OR BACK STAY

Long, slender turnings need to be supported and this can be done either by using some kind of mechanical steady or, as many professional turners do, by using hand pressure to apply an equal and opposite force to the cutting tool.

Wherever possible I much prefer to steady by hand, but on some projects it becomes extremely difficult to control the cutting tool with one hand. Such a project is the long-stemmed goblet, the final project in this book.

The sophisticated type of steady shown in Fig 2.8 was made by an engineer for metalworking purposes. Since acquiring it I find it is a great help on such slender turnings as the goblets. Many turners, however, make their own wooden steady.

No doubt you will acquire more and more equipment as time goes by. It is usually money well spent, particularly as it allows the turner to make an even greater range of pieces.

Chapter 3
Light Pulls

TIME: 20 MINUTES ★

I don't suppose there are many woodturners who have not, at some time or other, had a go at making these. There are several reasons for this: one is that they utilize scrap ends of wood that might otherwise be consigned to the firewood pile; another is that they can be 'fill in' jobs between more advanced projects; last but not least, they always sell well. The ability to produce them quickly also allows the maker to sell them at a very competitive price.

DESIGN CONSIDERATIONS

There is almost no limit to the variety of possible designs for light pulls. Fig 3.1 shows five completed pulls, and Fig 3.2 gives details of the different profiles, which readers may wish to copy or modify.

Fig 3.1 Five completed light pulls.

CHOICE AND PREPARATION OF STOCK

Most species of wood can be used, although I consider that the timbers best suited to light pulls are imported exotics and home-grown yew. Do not be deterred, however, if you only possess pine, oak, chestnut, etc. Many people have fitted bedrooms and kitchens in such species and are looking for a match. I have sold hundreds made in pine, while the acorn-shaped light pull can only really be made in oak!

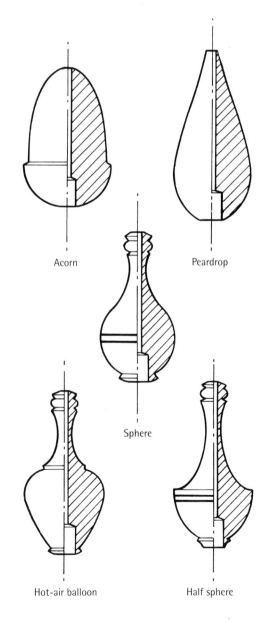

Acorn   Peardrop

Sphere

Hot-air balloon   Half sphere

Fig 3.2 Profiles of the suggested designs.

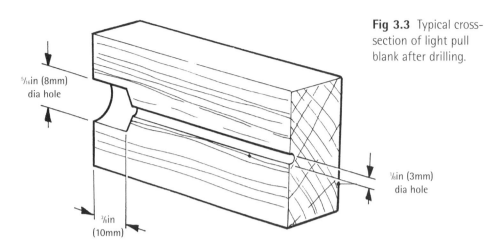

Fig 3.3 Typical cross-section of light pull blank after drilling.

⁵⁄₁₆in (8mm) dia hole

⅛in (3mm) dia hole

³⁄₈in (10mm)

Most of my light pulls are made from 1¼in (32mm) square stock, accurately dimensioned and cross cut to 2⅜in (60mm) in length. Next the holes are bored using two sizes of drill to suit the type of accessories that I prefer. At what will be the base of the pull, a hole ³⁄₈in (10mm) deep by ⁵⁄₁₆in (8mm) diameter is bored. The other end is drilled out with a ⅛in (3mm) hole going through to meet the larger hole (*see* Fig 3.3).

By using my pillar drill (*see* page 7), incorporating a simple jig clamped to the table, I avoid having to centre each length of stock.

The jig is simply a piece of MDF with two 45° angled cuts which provide a positive location and register for each piece and also prevent it spinning. **Caution:** do not attempt to bore large diameter holes by this method – it could be dangerous.

One blank only needs to be centred and punched. This allows the jig to be precisely located before clamping. Providing the stock has been accurately dimensioned and the ends cut square, all the other blanks can be drilled out, if sharp drills are used, with little effort (*see* Figs 3.4 and 3.5).

Fig 3.4 Boring jig set up ready for use.

Fig 3.5 Boring jig in use.

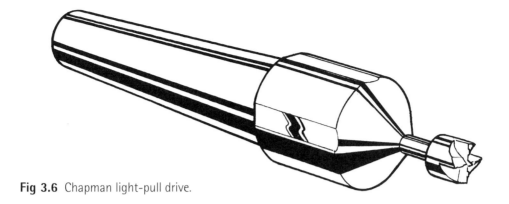

Fig 3.6 Chapman light-pull drive.

There are several ways of driving the stock and I shall describe two. I prefer to use a purpose-made drive in the headstock designed by Bob Chapman of Maidstone, Kent (*see* page 162). The four-prong hardened drive is $^5/_{16}$in (8mm) in diameter, but the shank is thinner (*see* Fig 3.6). With the blank pushed on to this drive it is possible to cut right down to the hole without damaging the tool edge on the drive. I find it best to use a 'dead' centre at the tailstock end for the same reason, applying a small amount of wax to prevent burning.

An alternative method is to use a small countersink bit mounted in a Jacobs chuck – most turners own both – allowing the same results to be achieved. By using either of these methods there will be no waste wood whatsoever! These accessories are shown in Fig 3.7.

ORDER OF WORK

The lathe can be run at about 2000rpm, and after initial roughing down to a cylinder I use one tool only to complete the whole profiling. This is a $^3/_8$in (10mm) spindle gouge ground with a longer than normal bevel and with the wings swept well back. I refer to this tool as my 'detail gouge', and it will facilitate the turning of other projects described later (*see* Fig 3.8).

A tool ground in this way will facilitate the cutting of tight intersections on any profile, but when forming a narrow fillet or a crisp intersection you must raise the back end of the tool handle considerably. This allows the extreme tip of the tool to complete the shaping. No other part of the tool could achieve this without fouling other parts of the profile (and risking a 'dig-in').

Remember that to cut a concave shape the gouge is presented on its side and rolled on to its back by the time it reaches the bottom of the intended shape. The opposite profile, the

Fig 3.7 Left: Chapman drive, right: Jacobs chuck with countersink bit.

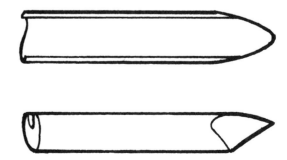

Fig 3.8 Profile of detail gouge.

convex, demands exactly opposite presentation and movements, i.e. present it very much on its back and then roll right over on to its side by the time it reaches the base of the intended shape. Fig 3.9 shows the gouge in use.

Some of my pulls are embellished with a couple of burn lines. These are achieved by making a slight nick in the required places with the toe of the skew chisel, followed by holding a length of cheese or piano wire in the grooves as the wood revolves (*see* Fig 3.10). **Caution:** do not be tempted to use a length of wire for this purpose unless it is secured at both ends to wooden toggles to grip on. It is dangerous!

Fig 3.10 Applying burn marks with piano wire. (Note that the wooden toggles attached to the ends of the wire for safety reasons are obscured in the photograph.)

FINISHING

I cannot think of any artefact made on a lathe that is handled more than a light pull, so the finish you apply must be durable. Friction polish or sealer is just not good enough, as the pull would quickly become dull and tatty. After sanding down to about 320 grit, a minimum of two coats of a hard, durable finish such as melamine or polyurethane should be applied.

Fig 3.9 Detail gouge in use.

Chapter 4

Toadstools

TIME: 35 MINUTES ★

These objects definitely rate in the best-selling category at the lower end of the market, and fall into the price range that many will buy on impulse. There is no doubt that a well-turned and highly polished toadstool, whether sold individually or arrayed in clusters on a piece of burr log, seems to fascinate the would-be buyer. A completed arrangement is shown in Fig 4.1.

Fig 4.1 'Planted' burr log.

DESIGN CONSIDERATIONS

Single, free-standing toadstools must have a base large enough to be stable. Many turners leave a natural edge at both top and bottom, thus ensuring maximum stability, while others turn a symmetrical base. Whatever you do, the base must not only look in proportion to the head, it must also be stable. Combining the two is sometimes not easily achieved.

The shape of the head or crown is left to the individual, and you have a certain amount of artistic licence to create as much visual impact as possible and also to show off the best features in the wood. The true mushroom shape is too regular and symmetrical for my liking, so I prefer the toadstool shape as shown in Fig 4.2. This shows the two different bases, that is, the natural edge and the symmetrical. It also shows the much smaller fungus-type shape which is rarely sold individually, but is used almost exclusively for 'planting' in a piece of log.

The larger type can also be 'planted', and obviously any shape so fixed must have a parallel portion turned at its base to fit into a corresponding size hole drilled in the log. The 'planting' must not be too regimental or the whole effect can be spoiled. I think that the smaller fungi look best coming off the log at an angle (as they very often do in nature). The overall effect can be improved dramatically if use is made of artificial heathers, grasses and flowers.

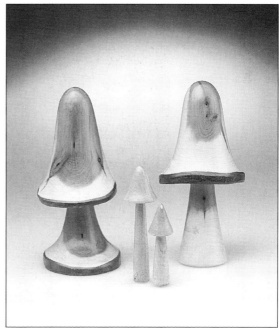

Fig 4.2 Typical profiles: left to right, toadstool with natural edge base, small fungi for 'planting', toadstool with turned base.

13

CHOICE AND PREPARATION OF STOCK

Yew wood branches are my favourite for the toadstools, as the contrasting colours of the sap and heartwood can provide stunning effects. Alternative woods that produce satisfactory results are laburnum, box and rhododendron. The smaller fungi are best made, in my view, from a lighter coloured wood such as holly or sycamore. Those shown in the photographs were made from maple, and after polishing they have taken on a near natural colour.

Inexperienced turners should not tackle yew wood limbs exceeding 3in (76mm) in diameter. The thicker the limb, the more difficult (and potentially dangerous) it becomes. Yew is a very dense and hard timber, and as mass increases so do the downward forces encountered when using a lathe, thus making the tools more difficult to control. I would suggest using branches between 2 and 3in (50–75mm) in diameter, though even these sizes may well be too large and look out of proportion if 'planted' in a log!

Because I make use of a spigot chuck to hold the stock, I normally cut the branches into lengths of about 4½in (114mm). If a screw chuck is your choice, it will be necessary to cut about 1in (25mm) longer to allow for parting off. Ideally, a dead straight piece of branch should be used, but procuring one is rare and wasteful. Do not despair, however, because pieces that are bent and irregular can be used by adopting the method shown in Fig 4.3 and described below.

After cutting the branch to length, guess the centres at both ends and pierce with a bradawl. Mount the stock between centres and, if using the spigot chuck, part in at the tailstock end to the appropriate diameter to fit the spigot. (If it is intended to use a screw chuck for the secondary fixing, slightly undercut the branch at the tailstock end down to about ⅛in/3mm diameter. Remove from the lathe, cut away the remaining nib with a gouge and make a suitable pilot hole in the centre of the still visible nib to suit the screw chuck.)

This procedure will ensure that when the stock is reversed and remounted on its secondary fixing it will be as balanced and symmetrical as it is possible to make it. The bent section in the middle of the piece will subsequently be turned away.

The maple used for the fungi shown in Figs 4.1 and 4.2 was prepared from 7in (178mm) lengths of 1in (25mm) square stock. These were mounted between centres and, after being reduced to a cylinder, a small spigot was cut at both ends to fit the appropriate size chuck. They were then bandsawn into two equal lengths, mounted in the chuck and profiled completely with the ⅜in (10mm) 'detail gouge' (*see* page 11).

Preparation of the log for 'planting' depends on individual taste. Some prefer to leave the

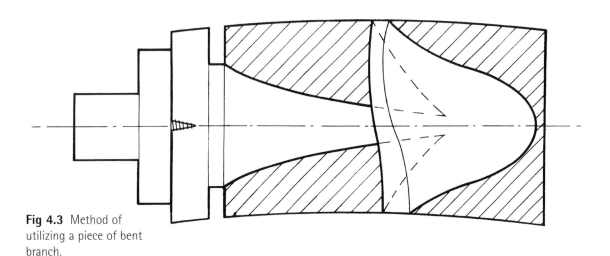

Fig 4.3 Method of utilizing a piece of bent branch.

Fig 4.4 Burr log prepared for 'planting'.

bark intact, others prefer to remove it. In all likelihood, in addition to harbouring 'creepy-crawly' things, it will come away eventually of its own accord. I always remove it with a carpenter's chisel and clean it off with a stiff wire brush and disinfectant. It should finish up looking something like the piece shown in Fig 4.4.

ORDER OF WORK

Reverse chuck the piece on to the spigot or screw chuck. I then recommend that the tailstock be brought up to give a little support and confidence. Now, with the lathe running at about 1500rpm, take a parting tool and set out (a) the overall length – one width of the tool and about ¼in (6mm) deep and (b) the point where the head and stalk merge. Go in here to about 1in (25mm) diameter and two or three parting tools wide (in the waste wood side).

At this stage the profiling of the head can commence. I use a small roughing-out gouge for most of the shaping, and refine and finish with a ⅜in (10mm) spindle gouge (*see* Fig 4.5).

Again making use of a small roughing-out gouge, remove the waste wood between the base and parting cuts defining the bottom of the head, taking care to leave a small portion of natural edge at the base of the stalk if so desired. The tailstock is now removed and the small pip at the very top of the toadstool can be turned off with a spindle gouge (*see* Fig 4.6).

Fig 4.6 The stem has been shaped (with tailstock support) and the pip at the top removed with the tailstock removed.

Fig 4.5 Initial sizing and profiling with tailstock support.

Fig 4.7 Commencing the undercutting with the 'toe' of the ½in (13mm) skew chisel – note that it is flat down on the tool rest for this operation.

Now to the most difficult part of the project. So as to ensure that an even amount of natural edge bark remains on the bottom of the head, it is necessary to undercut it. (Parting in at right angles to the stock would leave varying degrees of bark thickness and spoil the whole effect.)

The idea is to shape the first portion of the undercut parallel to the outside profile, and I make use of my ⅜in (10mm) 'detail gouge'. This is quite an advanced technique requiring no little nerve and experience, so I recommend the use of a flat section ½in (13mm) skew chisel (*see* Fig 4.7). (I advise against using the same size in the oval-section variety – it is too flimsy, and as the amount of tool overhang increases it becomes impossible to control, and may result in an almighty 'catch'.)

After this initial undercutting (which is done by using the tool scraper fashion), it is a matter of removing the remainder bit by bit. For this, use the long point to both undercut the head and also continue the taper on the stalk until they meet in a nice crisp intersection.

When the undercut nears the stalk, you will need to slightly tip the chisel on to its right-hand side (as viewed from the front of the lathe) or the heel will foul the stalk (*see* Fig 4.8).

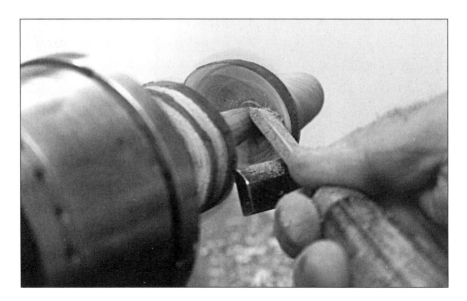

Fig 4.8 Continuing the cut to the intersection with the stalk. Note that the chisel has been tipped on to its right edge to avoid the heel fouling the stalk.

Remember, however, that if when tipped any part of the cutting edge other than the toe of the chisel engages the whirling wood, you will be offending one of the basic 'laws of woodturning' (see page 161) and again you could experience a hefty 'catch'.

It is inevitable that early efforts may well experience the odd 'dig-in' when undercutting, but do not be deterred. Perseverance and careful study of the recommended sequence of operations shown will eventually prove successful!

FINISHING

The project is now ready for sanding. Remove the tool rest and commence by smoothing the rough edges off the bark beneath the head *with the lathe stationary*.

Now start the lathe and, with pieces of abrasive torn into about 1in (25mm) strips, sand the head and the stalk, taking great care to avoid the ragged bark edges. Sanding the

undercut section and the stalk where it merges demands even greater concentration to avoid injury, and my method is to feed the abrasive into the desired areas and not my fingers.

When the sanding is complete, apply the finish with a small paintbrush (with the lathe stationary) which will ensure that all parts are reached. The lathe is then started and the whole is buffed up to a nice shine. Yew wood responds very well to friction polish, and if followed by an application of carnauba a fairly durable finish is attained.

The final stage is to part off, and if a newly sharpened tool is used an acceptable finish will be obtained.

Caution: the potential danger when sanding and polishing ragged bark edges cannot be overemphasized. Maximum concentration is required, and rather than use rags to polish I recommend the use of Liberon finishing cloths (see page 162). If they catch the ragged edge they will tear, rather than grab and trap the retaining fingers.

Chapter 5
Wooden Eggs

TIME: 30 MINUTES ★

I commented at the start of the previous project that yew wood toadstools fascinated the would-be buyer. It is true to say that well-turned and polished wooden eggs seem to hold an even greater fascination.

Wooden eggs are a highly collectable commodity and many people, both woodturners and non-turners, have amassed scores in different species of wood, often displaying them in specially designed cabinets. Fig 5.1 shows a selection of eggs in a wicker basket.

Fig 5.1 A display of eggs.

It is difficult to imagine a more tactile object than an egg being produced on a lathe. To hold a well-turned wooden egg can for many people impart a soothing, therapeutic effect. Indeed, some psychiatric units encourage patients to touch and caress them for these very reasons.

DESIGN CONSIDERATIONS

It is a great pity that many of the wooden eggs I see displayed at craft markets and the like are of such poor quality and shape. I accept that

Fig 5.2 Profile of preferred egg shape.

real eggs vary considerably in form: one only has to study a book on wild birds to see how their eggs vary from being almost a true sphere, as in the case of owl eggs, to the long, pointed contours of guillemot eggs. None, however, have ridges, flat spots or sudden changes of direction!

While I have included wooden eggs in the 'beginners' projects, a really well-shaped egg is far from easy to achieve. The shape of egg I prefer is the one shown in Fig 5.2. This was made several years ago and deliberately painted black to enable me to see the true form. When turning a run of eggs, this 'template' is always positioned on the lathe bench for constant reference. The size of my eggs ($2\frac{5}{8}$in/67mm long by $1\frac{3}{4}$in/44mm diameter at their thickest) is influenced by the fact that most exotic wood squares come in multiples of 3in (76mm), that is 12in (30.5cm), 18in (45.7cm) and 24in (61cm). If, therefore, the egg is produced from a 3in (76mm) long piece of wood, there will be little waste.

CHOICE AND PREPARATION OF STOCK

Almost any species of wood can be used, but the selling price of the egg is obviously influenced by the buying price of the stock. In the case of many of the exotics, this can be substantial. However, some of the best effects can be obtained by making use of the branches pruned from garden trees, such as rowan, cherry, sumach, laburnum, yew, plum, box, lilac, etc.

Preparation of the stock depends on your preferred method of chucking. The quickest and best turner of wooden eggs I know cuts his stock into 3in (76mm) lengths and turns it between centres, leaving a tiny nib at each end to be later machine sanded and buffed to a final finish.

My method of chucking uses the 1in (25mm) spigot of the O'Donnell jaws – part of the Axminster Power Tool Company Four-Jaw system – (*see* page 4), combined with a home-made wooden 'spring' chuck (*see* page 22).

ORDER OF WORK

Prepare by cutting the 2in (51mm) square-section stock (or similar sized branchwood) into 6in (152mm) lengths. These are then mounted between centres and reduced to a cylinder with a roughing gouge. A 1in (25mm) spigot is then formed at *both* ends with a parting tool (*see* Fig 5.3). On a production run, as many as 50 lengths would be so prepared.

The next stage is to cross-cut all these pieces into two equal lengths, leaving each 3in (76mm) piece ready to be secured in the spigot chuck.

Set the lathe at about 1500rpm, and begin by reducing the cylinder to slightly over the final diameter of 1¾in (44mm). Now, with a pencil held against the whirling wood, scribe a mark 2½in (64mm) from the open end and, with a narrow parting tool, size in to about ¾in (19mm) diameter in the waste wood side (left of the pencil line). Taking this sizing cut any deeper at this stage is not advisable, as chatter would probably be encountered when shaping.

Now scribe another pencil line ⅞in (22mm) in from this end to indicate the largest diameter and where the curves merge.

With a skew chisel or spindle gouge (I prefer the ½in/13mm skew), commence the profiling of the pointed end of the egg just slightly to the right of the pencil mark. Aim for a nice flowing action combined with the necessary lifting and swinging movements. If using a skew, it is more comfortable (but also more difficult) to use it left-handed. Used right-handed your body tends to get in the way, making the stance awkward. In either posture the whole of the shaping of this pointed end can be achieved with the heel or short point of the chisel pointing down.

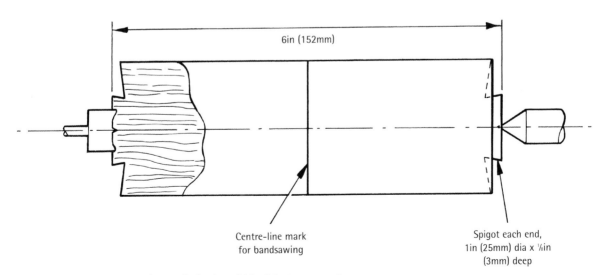

6in (152mm)

Centre-line mark
for bandsawing

Spigot each end,
1in (25mm) dia x ⅛in
(3mm) deep

Fig 5.3 Method of preparing a 6in (152mm) blank between centres.

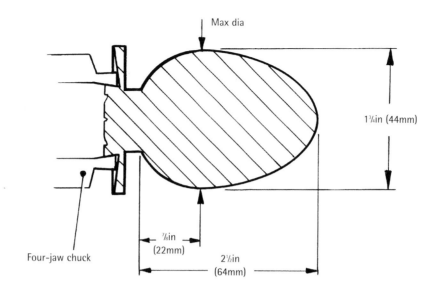

Fig 5.4 Initial shaping of the 3in (76mm) blank held in the spigot chuck.

The shaping of the blunt or rounded end can now proceed, starting this time to the left of the pencil mark. As the curve at this end is more rounded (*see* Fig 5.4), the gouge or chisel must be swung correspondingly 'quicker'.

When satisfied with the profile thus far, stop the lathe and check that the partly shaped egg fits to your satisfaction in the wooden 'spring' chuck. If it does, the completed area can be

sanded and polished. *Do not* part off at this stage.

The same process can now be repeated on several more blanks, which will give the polish time to harden before the next stage.

It is now time to reverse chuck the partially turned eggs, using a home-made wooden 'spring' chuck held in the O'Donnell jaws (*see* page 22 for constructional details of this chuck).

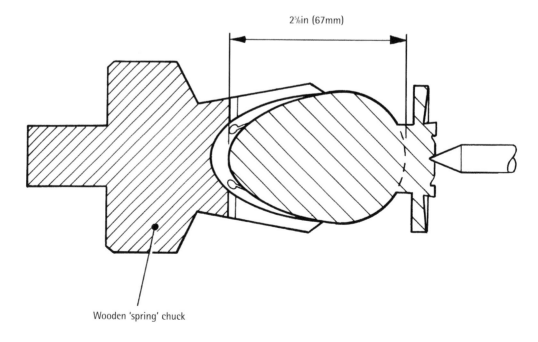

Fig 5.5 Part-turned egg reversed into the wooden 'spring' chuck.

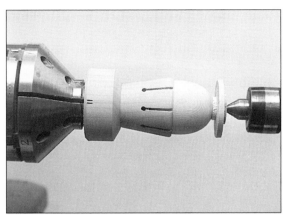

Fig 5.6 The part-turned egg in the wooden chuck. Note the two marks on the base of the 'spring' chuck lined up with two pop marks on the metal chuck.

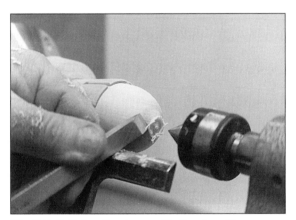

Fig 5.7 Refining the shape with the skew. The tailstock has been removed.

The partially turned egg is pushed centrally into the wooden chuck with the aid of the tailstock located in the centre mark still left on the face of the square end. This will ensure that the stock runs dead true and is the reason why I emphasized that you should not part off at the rounded end *before* reverse chucking (*see* Figs 5.5 and 5.6).

The tailstock can remain in place while most of the waste wood is removed, but obviously taken away for the final delicate finishing cuts. For these final cuts at the rounded end you will probably need to flick the chisel over and use the toe or long point of the chisel facing down, otherwise the handle of the tool would need to be lifted uncomfortably high (*see* Fig 5.7).

The swinging of the gouge, and more particularly the skew when used, must be timed perfectly to avoid being thrown upwards and backwards into the dreaded 'dig-in'. The heel of the bevel should glide on the area just cut. If the tool handle is not swung sufficiently, the cut comes off. If it is swung too quickly, the bevel contact is lost and a 'dig-in' occurs (*see* Fig 5.8). Perseverance, however, will bring its just rewards, so keep on trying.

Finally, sand and polish and remove the egg from the wooden chuck with a light tap, using the palm of the hand.

1 The tool handle has not been swung quickly enough to the right, resulting in the heel of the bevel preventing the tool from cutting.

2 The bevel is lined up with the heel gliding on the surface just cut.

3 The handle of the tool has been swung too quickly to the right. Bevel contact has been lost. The tool edge will be thrown upwards and backwards into a 'dig-in'.

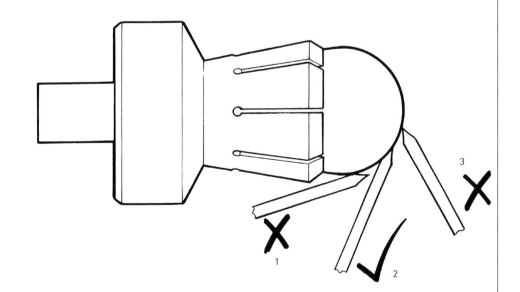

Fig 5.8 The importance of bevel rubbing.

FINISHING

This has already been touched on, and in a demonstration I would probably use a friction polish and paste wax. More durable finishes are available, however, such as oil and wax or melamine and wax. My production runs are spray-finished with a coat of sanding sealer followed by a top coat of a tough semi-gloss melamine lacquer.

CONSTRUCTION OF THE WOODEN 'SPRING' CHUCK

Constructional and dimensional details are as shown in Fig 5.9. It can be turned to suit your preferred metal chuck, and the outside shaped similar to the example in the drawing. The internal egg cup profile, which should be slightly less than 1¾in (44mm) diameter at its opening, is formed with gouge and scraper. The

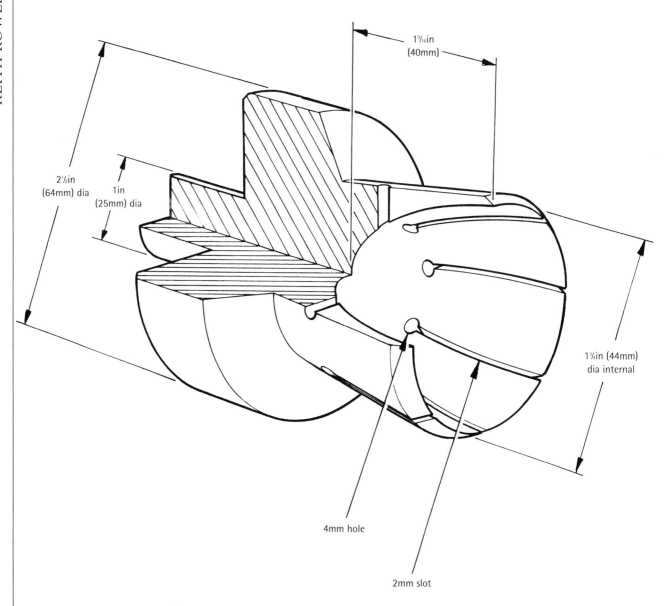

1⁹⁄₁₆in
(40mm)

2½in
(64mm) dia

1in
(25mm) dia

1¾in (44mm)
dia internal

4mm hole

2mm slot

Fig 5.9 A typical wooden 'spring' chuck.

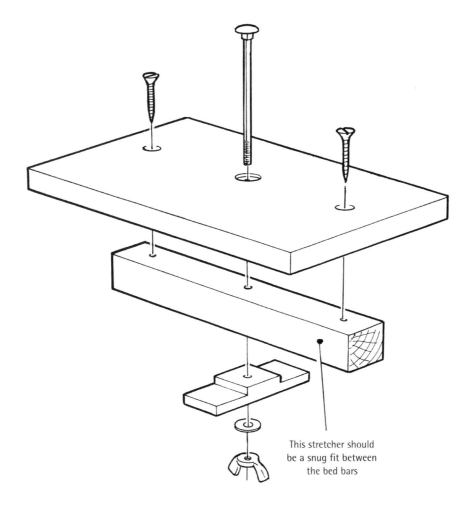

This stretcher should
be a snug fit between
the bed bars

Fig 5.10 A typical platform to facilitate the use of a router.

holes and slots are made with the help of a router used on a jig fitted to the lathe. This jig is constructed mainly from MDF and has many uses. It is also used later in the book and is well worth making.

Some turners use either a jubilee clip or a tapered wooden ring to make the egg more secure in the chuck, but I do not find it necessary.

The jig and method of fixing it to the lathe and the router to the carrier is simple, but of course the dimensions will have to be adjusted to suit your own lathe. The most important requirement is for the dead centre of the router cutter to be lined up with the dead centres of the lathe, otherwise the cuts will not be truly radial (*see* Figs 5.10 and 5.11).

I first saw this type of home-made jig and router carrier used by a professional

woodturner for fluting and reeding. The great advantage of this over the box-type jig is that it can be used to follow curved profiles.

My Myford Mystro lathe is equipped with a 24-spaced dividing facility, and every three spaces was utilized to router the eight equally spaced 4mm holes around the circumference of the chuck. This cutter was then replaced with a 2mm cutter to cut the slots (*see* Fig 5.12).

To ensure that the 'spring' chucks are always located in the same position in the spigot chuck (thus ensuring true running) they are marked with two pen lines which are lined up with two centre pop marks on the body of the metal chuck. These can be seen in Fig 5.6.

Some may think that this is all too much trouble, but I can assure you it will speed up your egg-making tremendously, and the router jig will prove invaluable.

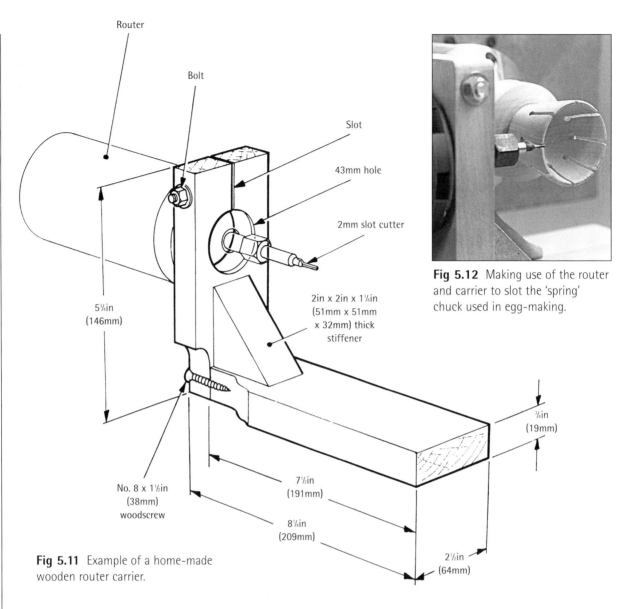

Router

Bolt

Slot

43mm hole

2mm slot cutter

5¾in
(146mm)

2in x 2in x 1¼in
(51mm x 51mm
x 32mm) thick
stiffener

No. 8 x 1½in
(38mm)
woodscrew

7½in
(191mm)

8¼in
(209mm)

¾in
(19mm)

2½in
(64mm)

Fig 5.11 Example of a home-made
wooden router carrier.

Fig 5.12 Making use of the router
and carrier to slot the 'spring'
chuck used in egg-making.

Chapter 6
Cheeseboard with Ceramic Tile Insert

TIME: 1 HOUR ★

This is another line at the lower end of the price range that has proved to be a good seller over the years. It is my experience that customers buy them not only to fulfil a functional purpose, but also to serve solely as a display piece for the kitchen.

DESIGN CONSIDERATIONS

So as to avoid the finished project being dominated by the 6in (152mm) ceramic tile, the base needs to be a minimum of 8½in (216mm) in diameter to allow for a generous 'border'. The handle must also be set at an angle to the base, otherwise the base would not sit flat and the user would have great difficulty in picking it up from a flat surface (*see* Figs 6.1 and 6.2).

Fig 6.1 The completed project.

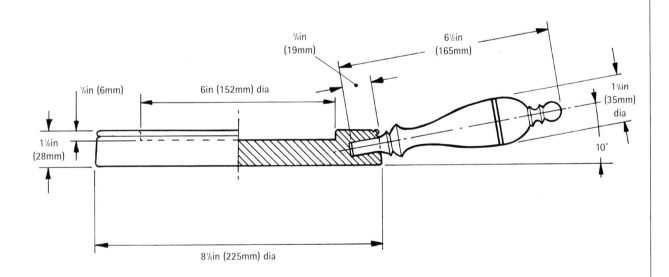

¾in (19mm)

6½in (165mm)

¼in (6mm)

6in (152mm) dia

1¾in (35mm) dia

1⅛in (28mm)

10°

8⅞in (225mm) dia

Fig 6.2 Constructional and design details.

CHOICE AND PREPARATION OF STOCK

For the best possible stability, I think it advisable to choose a piece of quarter-sawn stock (that is, where the annual growth rings of the tree run at right angles to the surface of the board). Some species are notorious for warping and these are best avoided.

Warping can be avoided to a great extent if, say, three pieces of 3in x 1in (76mm x 25mm) are glued edge to edge, and by arranging the annual rings in the centre piece to be opposite to the outside pieces. This is particularly necessary if you are working with, say, pine, which is very prone to warping badly if used in one solid width.

The choice of wood for this example was a piece of quarter-sawn English oak. The board, a full 1⅛in (28mm) thick, was planed true on one face and then marked out and cut to the required diameter on the bandsaw. The piece for the handle was obtained from a piece of 1½in (38mm) stock.

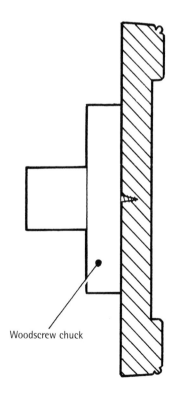

Woodscrew chuck

Fig 6.3 Method of chucking the base.

ORDER OF WORK

I started with the base and, after drilling the required size pilot hole, I mounted it on the new Craft Supplies Maxi-Grip 2000 chuck fitted with the woodscrew chuck accessory (*see* Fig 6.3).

The lathe speed was adjusted to about 1000rpm, and a ⅜in (10mm) bowl gouge was used to true up the edge and form the slight taper from base to top, as shown on the drawing. The tool rest can then be swung through 90° to be parallel with the face of the disc so that it can be trued up with the same tool.

The recess for the tile is now marked in, and I suggest that this is ⅛in (3mm) larger than the diameter of the tile. Failure to allow for movement in the wood will almost certainly result in a cracked tile. The recess is formed to the required depth with a parting tool and gouge, and flattened with a square-ended scraper or skew chisel (used scraper fashion). This recess needs to be dead flat, so it is advisable to check it with a straight edge. *It is dangerous to carry out this operation with the lathe spinning.*

I like to see a slight chamfer where the recess meets the 'border', and this can be done with a slicing cut using the long point of the skew. The same tool can then be used to form the small bead at the top corner of the base, partly by a cutting action and partly by scraping (*see* Fig 6.4).

The base, after being sanded, is now complete except for the boring of the ½in (13mm) hole to receive the handle, and it can now be removed from the lathe.

The blank for the handle is mounted between centres, and again I made use of the Chapman light-pull drive. This allows me to form the ½in (13mm) spigot at the very end of the blank without fouling the ⁵⁄₁₆in (8mm) diameter drive prongs.

The shape of the handle can be made to one's own liking and, after reducing the blank to a cylinder, the ½in (13mm) spigot to fit the hole is formed at the headstock end with a parting tool and aided by calipers. A good push fit is required!

Fig 6.4 Forming the bead on the edge of the base with a skew.

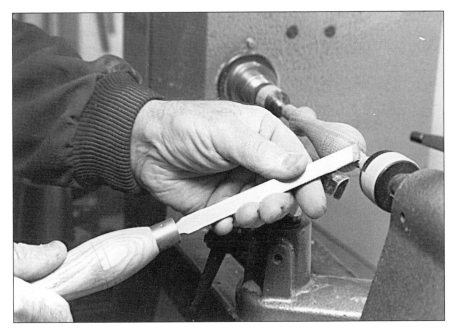

Fig 6.5 Refining the small sphere on the top of the handle with a skew.

Now, with chisel and gouges, your preferred handle profile can be fashioned (*see* Fig 6.5). Before completely parting off at the tailstock end it is advisable to remove it from the lathe and check the fit in a ½in (13mm) hole, and of course complete the sanding process.

The base now needs to be bored to take the handle. If you are only making a one-off then I suggest that a brace and bit or power drill is used. To assist in boring the hole at the correct angle, an adjustable bevel, set at 10°, can be

suitably positioned (*see* Fig 6.6). Extreme care must be taken to avoid making the hole too deep or you will break through the underside of the base.

For the amount of time it takes, I think it best (for those with a pillar drill) to make a drilling jig that takes away all the guesswork. The jig is of simple construction, and the two support pieces fixed at an angle of 45° ensure that the base always seats itself centrally on the jig. The depth stops on the pillar drill can also

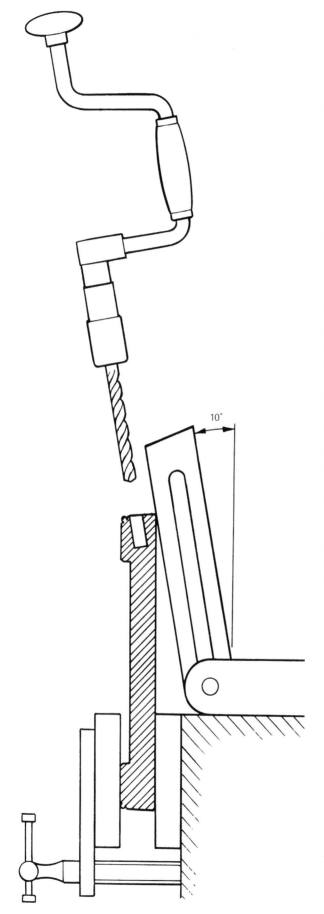

10°

be set to obviate the danger of bursting through the underside. Careful study of Figs 6.7 and 6.8 should make the construction of the jig fairly simple.

Before boring the hole, it is important to line up the grain of the base either vertically or horizontally (*see* Fig 6.8). Anything in-between will look dreadful! The handle can now be glued in position.

FINISHING

Because this project is intended for serving food, the choice of finish is limited. I think it best to apply several coats of Danish oil in accordance with the manufacturer's instructions. Do not oil the recess where the tile fits or the adhesive will not take.

The final operations are to fit an 8in (203mm) self-adhesive cork disc to the underside, and glue in the ceramic tile (three blobs of adhesive is adequate). I then affix a warning label, 'Do not immerse in water. Wipe clean with a damp cloth', on the underside.

Tiles, adhesive and cork discs are obtainable through several outlets (*see* page 162).

Fig 6.6 Making use of the adjustable bevel to drill at the desired angle of 10°.

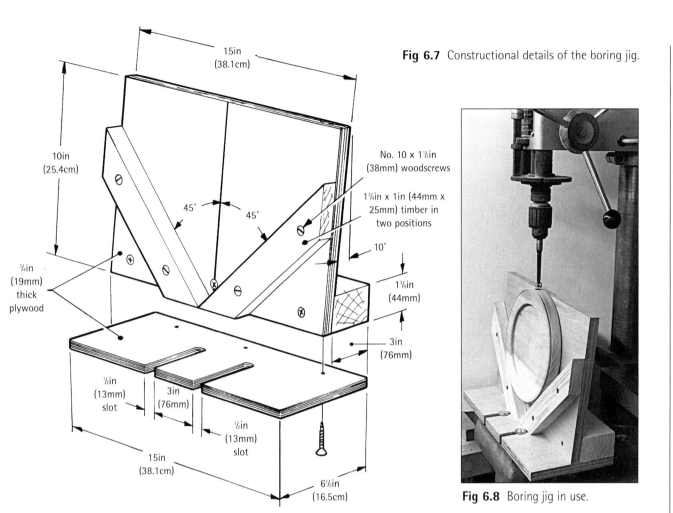

Fig 6.7 Constructional details of the boring jig.

15in
(38.1cm)

10in
(25.4cm)

45°   45°

¾in
(19mm)
thick
plywood

No. 10 x 1½in
(38mm) woodscrews

1¾in x 1in (44mm x
25mm) timber in
two positions

10°

1¾in
(44mm)

3in
(76mm)

½in
(13mm)
slot

3in
(76mm)

½in
(13mm)
slot

15in
(38.1cm)

6½in
(16.5cm)

Fig 6.8 Boring jig in use.

Chapter 7
Mug Tree

TIME: 2½ HOURS ★★

This project is suitable for making either on a production basis or, with a little more effort and planning, as a display piece.

DESIGN CONSIDERATIONS

The base must be of sufficient diameter and weight to ensure that the unit is stable when loaded, and I consider a 7in x 1¼in (178mm x 32mm) blank to be the optimum size. The first cross-piece must be positioned so that there is no likelihood of the bottom two mugs fouling the base. Many of the cheaper units have the cross-pegs leaving the stem at an upward angle, with the result that all the mugs gravitate and rest on the stem in an untidy display. This tree is designed so that the cross-pieces leave the stem at right angles, thus enabling the sometimes valuable china to be displayed to its best advantage.

Fig 7.1 The completed project.

CHOICE AND PREPARATION OF STOCK

For a production mug tree, virtually any species of wood from pine to oak can be used. For a tree intended as a display piece the choice can be a little more select, and a combination of contrasting woods can be used to add to the visual effect.

The choices for this example were padauk and ebony, which I feel go well together. The component parts are as shown in Figs 7.1 and 7.2, and should be studied carefully before commencing the project.

ORDER OF WORK

Commence by making the base. A pilot hole to take the screw chuck is drilled in the centre of the face that will eventually be the uppermost side.

After mounting on the chuck, and with the lathe spinning at approximately 1000rpm, the edge of the blank is trued up followed by the flattening of the face.

At this stage, form a spigot in the centre to fit into a 2in (51mm) spigot chuck. (The expanding jaws could also be used. In both cases the method of chucking will not be seen after subsequent reverse chucking and profiling.)

The blank can now be removed from the screw chuck and reversed on to the spigot. The Jacobs chuck, loaded with a ⅞in (22mm) cutter (I much prefer the sawtooth cutters for these operations) is fixed into the tailstock, and a hole to receive the stub tenon on the bottom of the stem is bored in the centre of the base to a depth of ¾in (19mm). The lathe speed should be reduced for this operation or the sawtooth cutter may overheat.

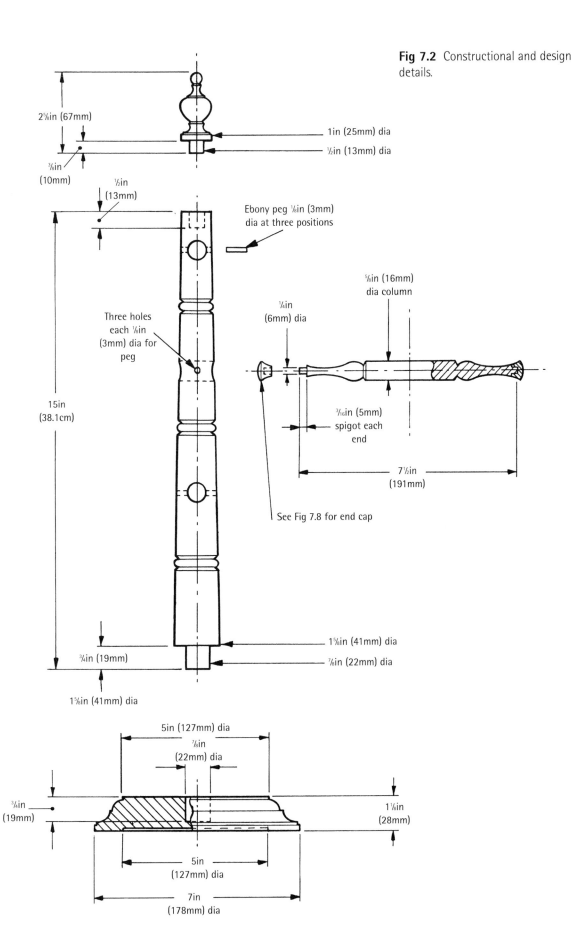

Fig 7.2 Constructional and design details.

2⅝in (67mm)

⅜in (10mm)

1in (25mm) dia

½in (13mm) dia

½in (13mm)

Ebony peg ⅛in (3mm) dia at three positions

Three holes each ⅛in (3mm) dia for peg

15in (38.1cm)

⅝in (16mm) dia column

¼in (6mm) dia

3/16in (5mm) spigot each end

See Fig 7.8 for end cap

7½in (191mm)

1⅝in (41mm) dia

⅞in (22mm) dia

¾in (19mm)

1⅝in (41mm) dia

5in (127mm) dia

⅞in (22mm) dia

¾in (19mm)

1⅛in (28mm)

5in (127mm) dia

7in (178mm) dia

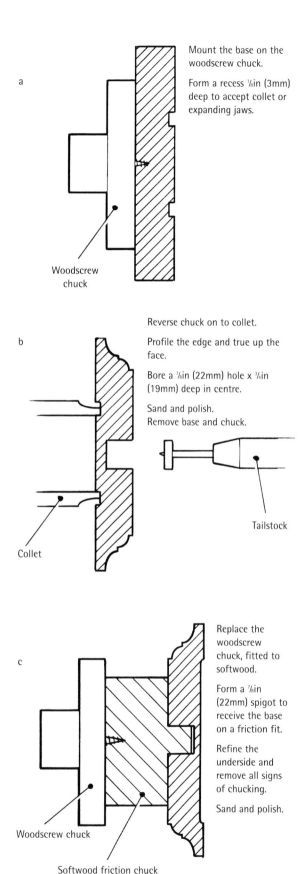

a

Mount the base on the woodscrew chuck.

Form a recess ⅛in (3mm) deep to accept collet or expanding jaws.

Woodscrew chuck

b

Reverse chuck on to collet.

Profile the edge and true up the face.

Bore a ⅞in (22mm) hole x ¾in (19mm) deep in centre.

Sand and polish.
Remove base and chuck.

Tailstock

Collet

c

Replace the woodscrew chuck, fitted to softwood.

Form a ⅞in (22mm) spigot to receive the base on a friction fit.

Refine the underside and remove all signs of chucking.

Sand and polish.

Woodscrew chuck

Softwood friction chuck

Fig 7.3 Sequence of chucking the base.

The profiling of the face and edge can now be done with gouges and scrapers, followed by sanding down to about 320 grit. If you intend to polish on the lathe, the face must be done now.

After allowing the polish to harden, remove the base from the spigot preparatory to the final reverse chucking. To do this, a piece of scrap wood can be fixed to a screw chuck on which a 1in (25mm) spigot is turned to receive the base on a good push fit. This enables all traces of the chucking system used to be turned away and makes sanding and polishing the underside much easier.

The sequence of chucking methods described above is clearly illustrated in Fig 7.3.

Next, prepare the stem or upright. For this the stock must be accurately planed, finishing at approximately 1½in (38mm) square. Mark out where the cross-pieces are located, and then gauge dead centre on these marks. It helps the subsequent drilling operation if the intersections of these marks are pricked with a pointed awl to provide positive location and prevent the drill from wandering off centre. Both ends of the stock also need to be similarly gauged and marked to ensure true running (*see* Fig 7.4).

The top of the stem is bored out with a ½in (13mm) hole to receive the spigot turned on the lower part of the finial (*see* Figs 7.2 and 7.5). This is done on the lathe, with the drill fixed in the Jacobs chuck and driven in the headstock.

Locate the end of the drill bit in the marked centre of the wood *with the lathe stationary*, and bring up the tailstock for alignment. Before starting the lathe, turn the stock by hand to give the drill a positive start. The lathe can now be started with the left hand preventing it from spinning and the right hand used to wind in the tailstock to the required depth. It may be advisable to get someone to switch the lathe on and off at your signal until you have gained some experience.

Caution: it is not advisable to bore holes much larger than this using this method. The attendant torque could twist the stock in your retaining left hand and cause injury.

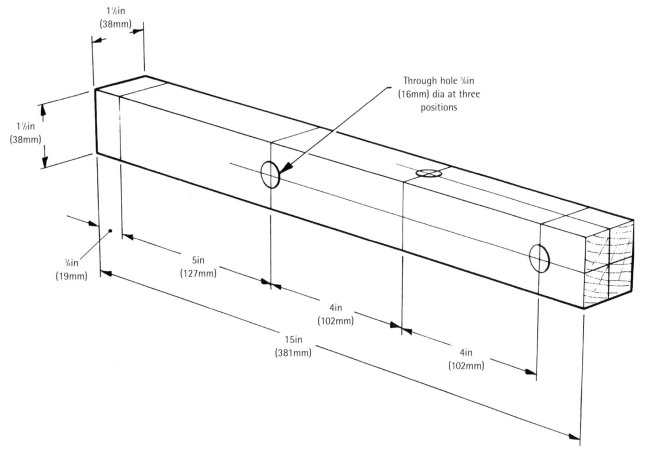

1½in
(38mm)

1½in
(38mm)

Through hole ⅝in
(16mm) dia at three
positions

¾in
(19mm)

5in
(127mm)

4in
(102mm)

15in
(381mm)

4in
(102mm)

Fig 7.4 Method of setting out the pillar and holes.

The three ⅝in (16mm) holes to take the cross-pieces or arms can now be bored. I do this in the pillar drill, but it can be done with a power drill or brace and bit, though care must be taken to minimize 'break-out' at the completion of the hole. Remember that the middle hole is bored at right angles to the other two.

The next step is to prepare the ebony finial. The stock is mounted between centres, reduced to a cylinder and a ½in (13mm) spigot formed at the tailstock end to fit the corresponding hole at the top of the stem.

'Dry' fit the partially turned finial to the stem, mount the whole between centres and commence the profiling. The spigot at the bottom is marked out and formed with a parting tool used in conjunction with calipers set to the required ⅞in (22mm) diameter. Make sure that the shoulder of the spigot is dead square or slightly undercut to ensure a good fit between base and stem.

The gentle taper between base and finial is then worked with a skew chisel, the same tool being used to form the three flush beads (*see* Fig 7.5). Almost all of the finial can now be shaped but, rather than trying to complete it at this stage by parting off, I suggest that you remove it from the main stem.

The tip of the finial can now be refined by preparing a scrapwood chuck (again fixed to the woodscrew chuck), boring a hole in the centre with a ½in (13mm) drill and jam fitting the finial into it. I consider this to be a superior method of finishing as opposed to 'manicuring' off the lathe (*see* Fig 7.6).

Before these three component parts are glued together, the ⅛in (3mm) holes to take the decorative ebony dowels (used to secure the three cross-pieces) are drilled. Great care must be taken to avoid 'break-out' or the stem will be ruined. My method is to drill the holes with the stem mounted between centres and the dividing head locked to prevent movement.

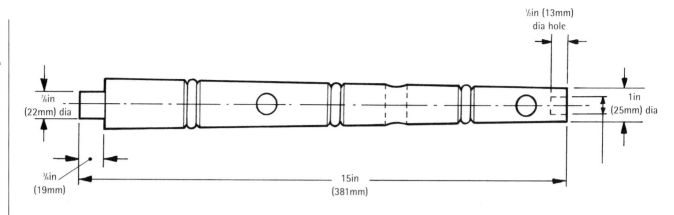

Fig 7.5 Completed pillar profile.

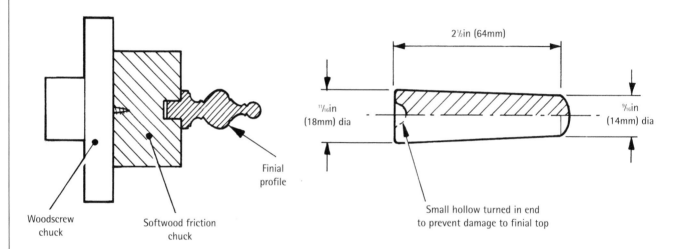

Woodscrew
chuck

Softwood friction
chuck

Finial
profile

Fig 7.6 Method of chucking the finial to facilitate refining cuts.

2½in (64mm)

¹¹⁄₁₆in
(18mm) dia

⁹⁄₁₆in
(14mm) dia

Small hollow turned in end
to prevent damage to finial top

Fig 7.7 Typical wooden morse taper plug used in the cramping and gluing process.

I make use of a dowel bit with a long point fixed in a hand-held wheel brace. By carefully observing the progress of the drilling it is possible to see the long point protrude through the back of the stem before 'break-out' occurs. It is then a simple matter to complete the hole from the other side.

Using the lathe as a cramp, the base, stem and finial are glued together. A large faceplate is fitted to the headstock and a wooden morse taper to the tailstock. A slight depression formed in the end of the latter prevents any damage to the ball at the top of the finial.

Minimal pressure only must be applied when winding the tailstock in to pull the joints together. Details of a typical wooden morse taper plug are shown in Fig 7.7.

The cross-pieces as can be seen from Fig 7.2, are turned in one length and fitted with a decorative ebony cap at each end. Prepare each piece to 7½in (191mm) long and ¾in (19mm) square, mount between centres and reduce the stock to a cylinder. Now cut a ¼in (6mm) diameter spigot at each end to receive the ebony caps. No further profiling is needed at this juncture. Prepare all three pieces to the same stage.

For the caps, six cubes of ebony (¾in/19mm on all sides) are prepared, centred on two opposite ends, and a ¼in (6mm) hole bored (in one end only) to fit on the corresponding spigots. Dry fit the cubes to the main arms, fix them between centres and complete almost all the profiling with roughing and spindle gouges.

Great care must be taken to ensure that these arms are a good fit in the ⅝in (16mm) holes in the stem. As with the finial, the refining cuts at the very end can best be done by friction fitting each cap onto a scrapwood spigot, so remove the part-turned caps from the arms and refine accordingly (*see* Fig 7.8).

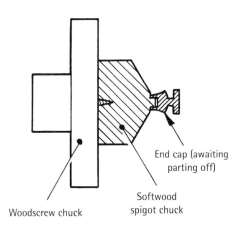

Fig 7.8 Method of chucking the end caps to facilitate parting and refining cuts.

Woodscrew chuck

End cap (awaiting parting off)

Softwood spigot chuck

A dab of glue in the hole of each cap will ensure a good fixing to the main arm. Cramp up in the lathe using wooden morse taper plugs in the headstock and tailstock. Allow the glue to set, and then the arms can be located in the stem, followed by the drilling of the ⅛in (3mm) holes to take the ebony dowels. These can be turned in one length or individually.

Finally, fit the dowels with a dab of glue, trim them off with a fine saw and then blend in to the profile of the stem by sanding *along the grain*.

FINISHING

You may prefer to apply your choice of finish as each component is completed. An alternative is to apply the finish when the tree has been assembled. I choose to spray-polish the piece with a sanding base coat which, after being cut back with very fine paper, is finished with wax and 'elbow grease'.

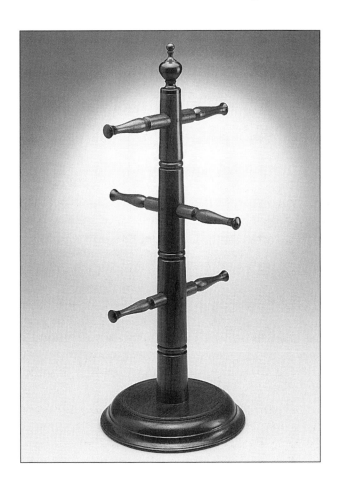

Chapter 8
Earring Stand

TIME: 1½ HOURS ★★

These little novelties are confirmed good sellers. Being modestly priced many will buy on impulse, particularly if the stand is attractively designed and well polished. The finished product is shown in Fig 8.1.

Fig 8.1 The finished project.

DESIGN CONSIDERATIONS

The 24 x ⅛in (3mm) holes bored in the earring-carrier should not exceed ³⁄₁₆in (5mm) from their centres to the edge of the disc, otherwise it will prove difficult for the hooks on the earrings to engage the hole. For the same reason the thickness of the wood at the hole locations should not exceed the same measurement.

I think it advisable to avoid profiling the finial to a sharp point as it is capable of inflicting a nasty puncture wound.

The ³⁄₈in (10mm) holes bored in the centre of the base and earring-carrier not only receive the corresponding spigots turned on the pillar and finial but also provide the means of chucking them for profiling (i.e., on a scrapwood friction-drive chuck, as illustrated in Fig 7.8 of the mug tree project).

The profiling of the components can be varied from my example as long as proportion and nice flowing curves are incorporated in the design.

Another important requirement is for the joints to be a precise push fit.

Figs 8.2 and 8.3 provide dimensional and constructional details, and you should look carefully at these before proceeding.

CHOICE AND PREPARATION OF STOCK

The choice of wood is left to individual preference, but of the home-grown species I prefer yew wood. Most of the exotics are obviously suitable, as are woods of contrasting colour.

The central pillar is prepared from ¾in (19mm) square stock and cut to a length of approximately 5³⁄₈in (137mm) long, accurately centred at both ends. The Chapman light-pull drive can again be put to good use to drive the pillar, as the diameter of the drive is less than the diameter of the tenon.

I make use of two templates to mark out the base and earring-carrier. These are made from ⅛in (3mm) plywood and cut to the required diameters, 3in (76mm) and 2³⁄₈in (67mm) respectively. Each has a small hole dead centre that will take a pointed awl.

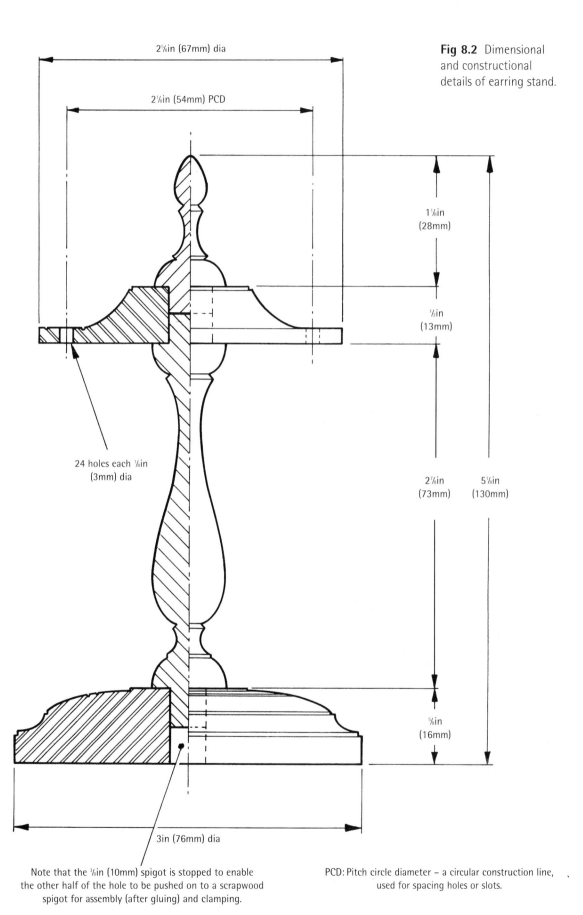

2⅝in (67mm) dia

2⅛in (54mm) PCD

Fig 8.2 Dimensional and constructional details of earring stand.

1⅛in (28mm)

½in (13mm)

2⅞in (73mm)

5⅛in (130mm)

24 holes each ⅛in (3mm) dia

⅝in (16mm)

3in (76mm) dia

Note that the ⅜in (10mm) spigot is stopped to enable the other half of the hole to be pushed on to a scrapwood spigot for assembly (after gluing) and clamping.

PCD: Pitch circle diameter – a circular construction line, used for spacing holes or slots.

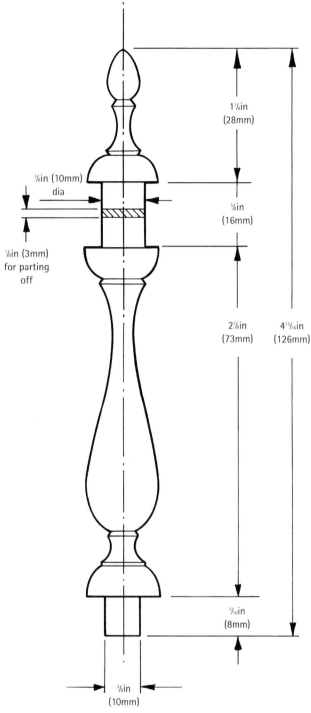

Fig 8.3 Dimensional and constructional details of earring stand pillar.

1⅛in (28mm)

⅜in (10mm) dia

⅝in (16mm)

⅛in (3mm) for parting off

2⅞in (73mm)

4¹⁵⁄₁₆in (126mm)

⁵⁄₁₆in (8mm)

⅜in (10mm)

The smaller pieces intended for the earring-carrier now require the 24 x ⅛in (3mm) holes drilling in them. To simplify this process I use a metal jig as shown in Fig 8.4. It will be seen that on the underside of the jig there is a steel peg (⅜in/10mm diameter) which locates in the hole in the earring-carrier, enabling the holes to be accurately and speedily drilled. After drilling the first hole, it is advisable to insert a steel peg or nail into the hole to prevent the wood from moving. Fig 8.5 shows the jig in use on the pillar drill, though a hand power drill could also be used if the wood is well clamped.

Fig 8.4 Metal drilling jig. The ⅜in (10mm) diameter pin for location in the corresponding hole in the wood can be clearly seen.

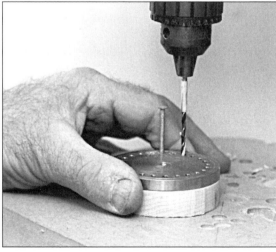

Fig 8.5 The jig in use. Note the nail that has been inserted in the first hole drilled to prevent the wood moving.

Plane the stock to the required thickness (⅝in/16mm and ½in/13mm respectively) and mark out the diameters with the aid of the templates, pricking the centre with an awl. Continue by bandsawing to size, then bore a ⅜in (10mm) through hole in each piece.

ORDER OF WORK

Mount a piece of scrap wood on a screw chuck, and with the lathe set at about 2000rpm reduce it to a cylinder and form a spigot ³⁄₈in (10mm) diameter by ⁵⁄₁₆in (8mm) long to receive the carrier on a good push fit. All the turning on this project can be done at the same speed.

Shape the blank to your liking using a ³⁄₈in (10mm) spindle gouge well over on its side and pulled from the centre towards the edge (with the grain), and with a swinging movement to form the concave profile (*see* Fig 8.6).

Make sure that the narrow area in the centre is dead flat or, better still, slightly hollow, ensuring a good joint with the shoulder to be formed on the finial. This can be done with a skew chisel used scraper fashion, as can the slight V cuts either side of the holes. A narrow parting tool is ideal to form the square fillet at the intersection of the curve and the flat near the centre. Sand down to about 320 grit and apply a coat of sealer or friction polish.

Repeat the process with the base and, again, only the three tools are required.

Fig 8.6 With the drilling process complete, the carrier has been mounted on a scrapwood spigot (fixed to the screw chuck), and is being profiled with a ³⁄₈in (10mm) spindle gouge. Note that the cutting is 'downhill', and with the grain.

Mount the prepared pillar blank between centres, reduce it to a cylinder and set out the position of the bottom and central spigots (the latter will subsequently be parted or sawn through). This setting out is perhaps best done with the aid of a marking stick, as shown in Fig 8.7.

Making use of a ¹⁄₈in (3mm) parting tool and calipers set to ³⁄₈in (10mm), size in as shown in Fig 8.7. It is important to leave the wood between the sizing cuts (near the top) intact to provide maximum stability when shaping the rest of the pillar.

The desired profiles can now be worked and I use one tool only, my ³⁄₈in (10mm) 'detail gouge' (*see* page 11). Sand and polish; at this stage the pillar should be similar to that depicted in Fig 8.8.

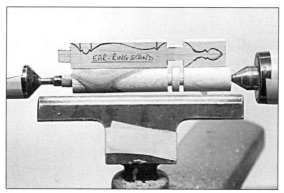

Fig 8.7 The pillar blank has been turned to a cylinder, with the spigots set out with the marking stick and sized in with a ¹⁄₈in (3mm) parting tool. Note the Chapman drive in use.

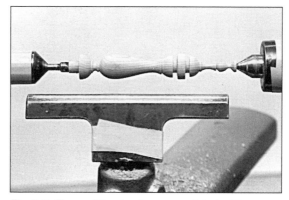

Fig 8.8 The profiling has been completed with one tool only, i.e. the ³⁄₈in (10mm) detail gouge. Note that waste wood between the parting cuts (near the top) has been deliberately left to provide stability.

The waste wood on the top spigot can now be removed with care and sized to the required ³⁄₈in (10mm) diameter with the ¹⁄₈in (3mm) parting tool and with the aid of calipers, as shown in Fig 8.9. The same tool can now be used to commence the parting off in the centre of the spigot. Fig 8.10 shows the pillar completed to this particular stage. (I do not think it advisable to part right through. It is safer and less likely to cause damage to the pillar if a fine-toothed handsaw or hacksaw blade is used with the lathe switched off.)

Test fit the pillar and finial joints. If overtight I use a small flat file to trim the spigots until a satisfactory joint is obtained (it is necessary to grind the file to remove the serrations on its edges or it is likely the shoulders of the spigots would be damaged).

Commence the gluing and clamping operation. To accomplish this, I again make use of the scrapwood spigot chuck to drive the glued and assembled stand. It is also necessary to use a wooden morse taper plug in the tailstock to apply the required clamping pressure (the plug is shown in Fig 7.7 of the mug tree project, page 34). This prevents the likelihood of splitting the finial, as would probably happen if a live centre was used. Fig 8.11 shows clearly the use of these 'accessories' in the clamping operation.

Fig 8.10 The parting-off position has been set with the parting tool before the suggested cutting off with a fine handsaw.

After allowing a few minutes for the glue to grab (and this is all the time that is required if the joints are good), the whole project can be lightly sanded to remove any nibs on the previously applied sealer/polish. **Caution:** do not start the lathe with the clamping pressure still applied. The attendant torque would probably twist and break the pillar at its smallest diameters! The final coats of polish can now be applied.

The final shaping and parting off at the finial end is perhaps most easily effected with a small skew chisel, and it will be necessary, as shown in Fig 8.12, to support the whirling stand with the left hand while doing so. With the left hand still lightly supporting the stand, remove the tailstock and blend in the extreme tip of the finial (with the lathe running) with some fine-grade abrasive.

Now apply a final dab of polish.

FINISHING

Unless you have applied your choice of finish to each component as it is completed, follow the procedure outlined for the mug tree on page 35.

The project is completed by neatly fixing self-adhesive baize to the underside of the base.

Fig 8.9 The same waste wood being removed with a ¹⁄₈in (3mm) parting tool, and being calipered to the required diameter.

Fig 8.11 Making use of the lathe to clamp the glued and assembled stand together. Note the wooden morse taper plug inserted in the tailstock, and the scrapwood spigot attached to the woodscrew chuck.

Fig 8.12 Final parting off at the finial end. Note how close the tool rest is positioned for optimum support and how the left hand lightly cradles the whirling wood.

Chapter 9
Finger-ring Stand

TIME: 1½ HOURS ★★

This is a very similar project to the earring stand, and they are almost as popular with the buying public. Give or take a few minutes, they require about the same length of time to make so the asking price can be the same.

DESIGN CONSIDERATIONS

Making the overall height the same as the earring stand gives the bonus of being able to sell them in pairs, and this sometimes stimulates sales, particularly if a concession on price is made for buying both together.

The rings are obviously intended to suspend on the flat areas between the beads (it is important that the beads should not exceed ⁷⁄₁₆in/11mm in diameter or the smaller children's rings will not pass over them). On this particular design the bulbous swell on the pillar is the opposite way round to the earring stand, which I think is a pleasing contrast.

The photograph of the finished project (Fig 9.1) and the diagrams (Figs 9.2, 9.3 and 9.4) should be studied carefully before making a start.

CHOICE AND PREPARATION OF STOCK

The choices of wood described for the earring stand also apply to this project.

The base is identical to the earring stand, and accordingly it is similarly prepared. The pillar is also from stock of the same dimensions but, in addition to it being accurately dimensioned and centred at both ends, a ⁷⁄₃₂in (5.5mm) hole needs to be drilled near the intended finial end to receive the cross-pieces.

As with the previous project, I think it advisable to prepare a marking stick which will

Fig 9.1 The completed project.

simplify the setting-out of the hole centre and the profile details. Fig 9.5 shows such a stick in use.

The hole is perhaps best drilled before any turning commences, and I use the pillar drill for this purpose.

The two arms are prepared from ½in (13mm) square section to a length of approximately 2¼in (57mm), accurately centred at both ends for between-centres turning.

ORDER OF WORK

The making of the base should follow exactly the same methods described in the making of the base for the earring stand (*see* page 39).

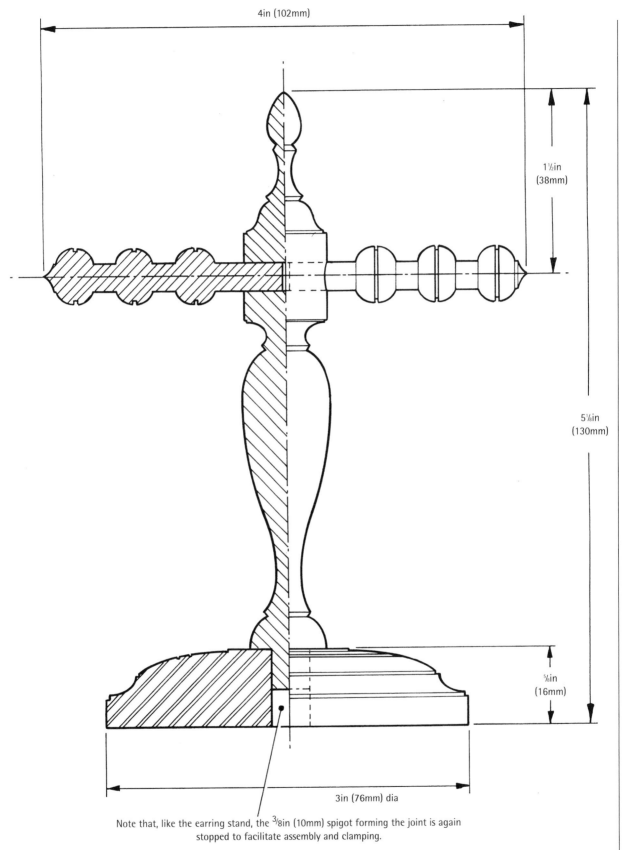

4in (102mm)

1½in (38mm)

5⅛in (130mm)

⅝in (16mm)

3in (76mm) dia

Note that, like the earring stand, the ³/8in (10mm) spigot forming the joint is again stopped to facilitate assembly and clamping.

Fig 9.2 Dimensional and constructional details of finger-ring stand.

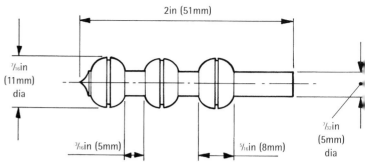

Fig 9.4 Dimensional details of the arms.

2in (51mm)

⁷⁄₁₆in (11mm) dia

³⁄₁₆in (5mm)

⁵⁄₁₆in (8mm)

⁷⁄₃₂in (5mm) dia

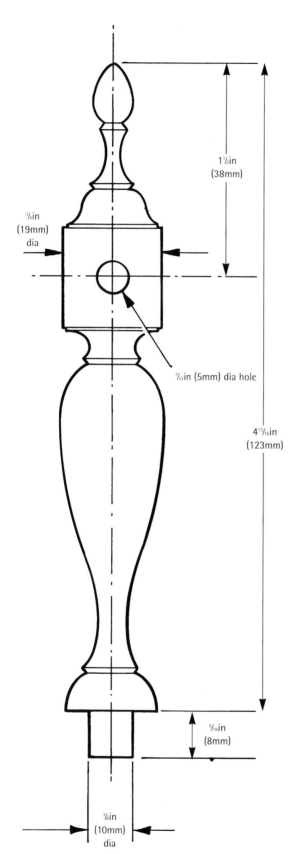

1½in (38mm)

³⁄₄in (19mm) dia

⁷⁄₃₂in (5mm) dia hole

4¹³⁄₁₆in (123mm)

⁵⁄₁₆in (8mm)

³⁄₈in (10mm) dia

Fig 9.3 Dimensional details of central pillar.

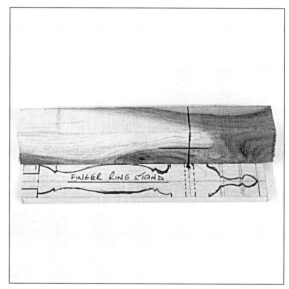

FINGER RING STAND

Fig 9.5 A marking stick being used to set out the hole centre.

The pillar, too, is a similar sequence. After the roughing down process, the marking stick (*see* Fig 9.5) should be used to set out the design features, followed by sizing in of the bottom spigot and general profiling. Remember to leave a small amount of waste wood at the finial end to fit in the wooden morse taper plug. This will enable the gluing and clamping process (on the lathe) to be done without any damage to the tip of the finial.

The two arms are turned between centres, use again being made of the Chapman light-pull drive. Turn the squares to a cylinder and then, with the aid of a previously prepared marking stick, set out the profile details on the whirling wood. Fig 9.6 clearly shows the method.

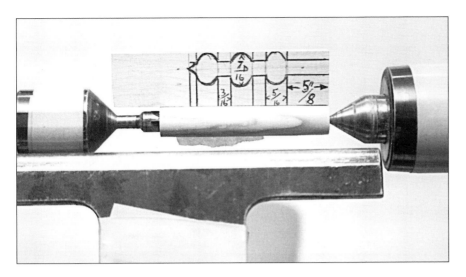

Fig 9.6 A marking stick being used to set out the arm profile.

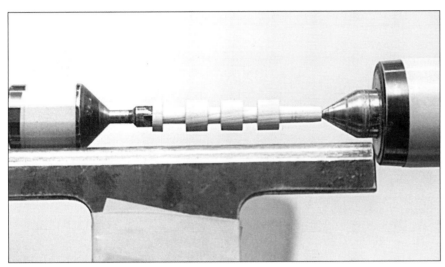

Fig 9.7 How the arm should look after the sizing-in process.

Continue now by sizing in to the required diameter of ⁷⁄₃₂in (5.5mm) to form the spigot for the joint and between the beads. The arm should now look like the profile shown in Fig 9.7. The beads can now be formed (I used the 'detail gouge'), followed by the sanding process.

Many turners would now part off at the headstock end and 'manicure' the end by hand methods. I prefer to do all the work on the lathe wherever possible, and this is the way I go about it.

Mount a piece of scrapwood on the screw chuck, reduce it to a cylinder and face off the open end with a gouge or chisel. Now bring up the tailstock and prick dead centre. Making use of a Jacobs chuck and the appropriate size drill (fitted in the tailstock), bore a hole to take the arm spigot on a tight fit. Fig 9.8 shows the

scrapwood chuck immediately after the boring operation, and Fig 9.9 shows the arm located (I used the tailstock centre to push the arm in, thus ensuring true running).

Fig 9.8 Typical scrapwood chuck, bored to accept the arm spigot.

45

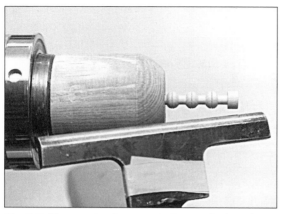

Fig 9.9 The arm has been pushed centrally into the chuck with the help of the tailstock to ensure true running.

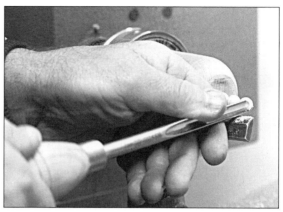

Fig 9.10 The profile at the very tip of the arm is being refined with the 'detail gouge'.

Fig 9.10 shows the very tip of the arm being refined with the 'detail gouge'.

After checking that all the component parts fit satisfactorily, the pillar can be glued to the base and clamped up in the lathe using the methods described in the making of the earring stand (*see* page 40). The arms are glued in by applying hand pressure.

FINISHING

This can be applied as each component part is made or after assembly, depending on the chosen finish. Both this and the earring stand are frequently handled, and ideally a durable finish is required to prevent the stands quickly taking on a tatty appearance.

Chapter 10
Salad Bowl and Servers

TIME: 3½ HOURS ★★★

There is no doubt that the general public's perception of a woodturner is someone who makes wooden bowls and very little else, and there are many who judge a turner's merit on his ability to produce good-quality bowls.

This is a great pity, because I take the view that just as much skill is required (and arguably more) to be a good spindle-turner as it is to be a good faceplate turner. There are some, of course, who are extremely competent at both, and I feel that relatively inexperienced turners should devote equal time to develop both disciplines.

DESIGN CONSIDERATIONS

Salad bowls are produced by the hundred and it could be argued that, being a purely functional item, they deserve little attention as to the question of design.

However, common faults are over-thick walls and bases, lack of any balanced form and sadly, in many cases, scant regard for the 'finish'.

Stability is one of the major considerations, and base size is critical. Too small and the bowl will be unstable. Too large and the design of the sides is limited. A good rule of thumb is to make the base not less than 33% of the largest diameter and certainly not more than 60%. The larger the base the straighter the profile will have to be, resulting in short (weaker) grained sides, and the shape will look clumsy, heavy and lifeless.

I hope that my example, 14in (356mm) diameter, 5in (127mm) thick, with a base of 6in (152mm) satisfies the criteria for both stability and visual appeal.

To complement the bowl, I have also described the making of a set of wooden salad servers so as to keep your spindle-turning skills

honed. For those wishing to purchase stainless steel 'business ends', I also describe the turning of suitable wooden handles and the method of fixing them.

The completed bowl and both sets of servers are shown in Fig 10.1.

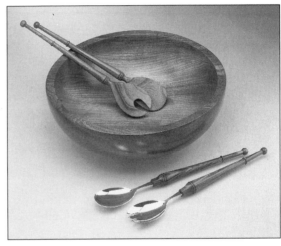

Fig 10.1 The completed bowl and two sets of salad servers.

CHOICE AND PREPARATION OF STOCK

Personal choice dictates the species of wood to be used for the bowl. Sycamore, ash and elm are eminently suitable, being obtainable in substantial dimensions. The example shown is a particularly nice piece of northern or wych elm. The all-wood servers are made from the same species, but the handles of the stainless steel servers are made in exotic tulip wood.

Salad bowls should ideally be no less than 12in x 4in (305mm x 102mm) deep, and I used a blank, 14in x 5in (356mm x 127mm) thick, which was well seasoned. The elm servers were accurately dimensioned to 1in x 2½in

(25mm x 64mm) and cut to lengths of 13in (330mm). The tulip wood blanks can be made from 1in (25mm) square section and cut to a length of 9in (229mm).

ORDER OF WORK

My preferred method of chucking for bowls of this size is to initially mount the blank on a 4in (102mm) faceplate, followed by reverse chucking onto the 3½in (89mm) expanding jaws of the Craft Supplies Precision Combination Chuck (*see* page 5).

The sequence is shown in Figs 10.2, 10.3 and 10.4.

Caution: a large piece of wood set at too high a running speed can be dangerous. Always err on the side of safety: the speed can be increased when the blank has been brought into balance. I start cutting from base to top (with the grain) with a ½in (13mm) bowl gouge turned well onto its side, and with the flute of the tool facing the direction of cut.

To obtain a nice flowing profile, balance and positioning of your feet are important, otherwise it will be difficult to achieve the necessary long, unbroken body movements. The base was flattened over a width of 6in (152mm), and a dovetailed recess 3½in (89mm) deep was worked with a parting tool and ½in (13mm) skew to accommodate the 3½in (89mm) expanding jaws.

After completing the profile to your satisfaction the outside of the bowl can be lightly scraped and sanded, commencing with about 80 grit through to about 320 grit (power sanding is much quicker and easier!). I make use of a proprietory brand of finishing oil, applying just one coat at this stage, burnishing almost immediately with a handful of elm shavings.

Before removing from the lathe, true up the back face of the blank (onto which the faceplate is fixed) to a depth of about 1in (25mm) with a spindle gouge (though a heavy-section beading tool is an easier and safer tool to employ). This procedure can be of great help in trueing up the blank after reverse chucking, as will be described below.

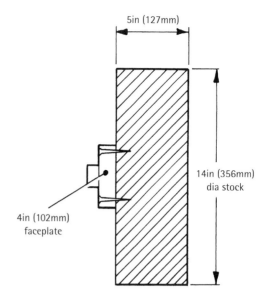

Fig 10.2 The blank has been mounted on a 4in (102mm) faceplate and secured with four screws.

5in (127mm)

14in (356mm) dia stock

4in (102mm) faceplate

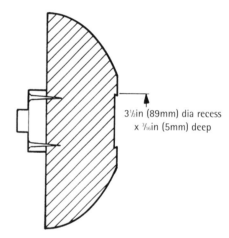

Fig 10.3 The outside profile has been shaped, together with the dovetailed recess, to take the 3½in (89mm) expanding jaws.

3½in (89mm) dia recess x ³⁄₁₆in (5mm) deep

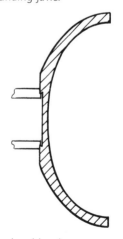

Fig 10.4 The bowl has been reverse chucked and the inside has been gouged out.

With the bowl reverse chucked on the expanding jaws and safely secured, start the lathe and check for true running. You will be lucky if it runs exactly true first time. With the tool rest close in, hold a pencil on the rest and mark the blank on the area that was trued up on the initial fixing and described in the previous paragraph. Stop the lathe, and you will see that the pencil has only marked the high side. Tap the centre area of this mark with a mallet and try again. A little perseverance will ensure absolute true running.

Hollowing out can commence with the same $\frac{1}{2}$in (13mm) bowl gouge, and the recommended grinding angle of 55–60° will cope adequately with this shape of bowl without any undue bouncing if the heel of the bevel glides on the surface of the area just cut. Initial cuts are made near the centre, always working from large to small diameter. As the cutting gets closer to the edge of the bowl, the peripheral speed increases, demanding positive entry to prevent the gouge being thrown outwards and thus damaging the rim.

Fig 10.5 shows the bowl gouge in use on the inside of the bowl, and Fig 10.6 illustrates the suggested completed profile and cross-section.

For a bowl of this diameter, I think a finished wall thickness of $\frac{5}{8}$in (16mm) is appropriate, so cutting should finish at slightly over this to allow for power sanding. When the desired surface finish has been achieved, apply a coat of finishing oil and burnish in with a

Fig 10.5 The bowl gouge in use on the inside of the bowl. Note that the rest is positioned as close as possible to assist tool control.

handful of shavings. The oiling process should be repeated three or four times, with an interval of 24 hours between each application. Each dried coat should be very lightly cut back with, say, 600 grit wet or dry abrasive. This method of chucking makes for quick fixing and removal from the lathe to carry out the oiling process. You should now have a nice-looking salad bowl with a pleasing, durable sheen.

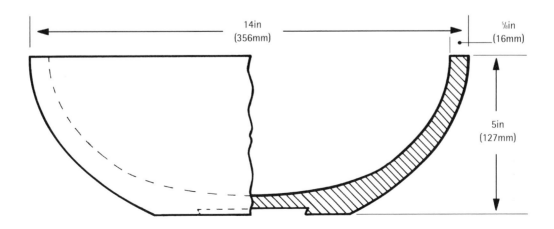

14in
(356mm)

⅝in
(16mm)

5in
(127mm)

Fig 10.6 The completed bowl profile with cross-section.

SALAD SERVERS

Before proceeding, the sequential drawings (Figs 10.7–10.14) should be studied as carefully as possible. All the necessary dimensions are provided, and strict adherence to the order of work will minimize the danger when using the bandsaw to cut the curved profile at the spoon end.

After the setting out of the blank (note the gauge marks on the centre of edge and face, Fig 10.7) and the initial bandsawing shown in Fig 10.8, the blank is mounted between centres and a 1in (25mm) diameter spigot (3in/76mm long) is formed. This end will subsequently fit into the 1in (25mm) spigot jaws.

The blank will now look like that shown in Fig 10.9, the curved profile of the spoon having

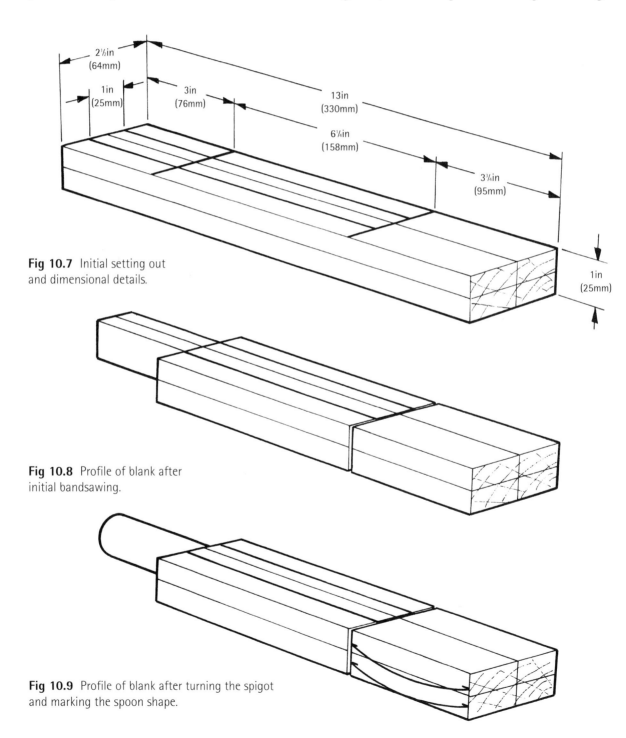

Fig 10.7 Initial setting out and dimensional details.

Fig 10.8 Profile of blank after initial bandsawing.

Fig 10.9 Profile of blank after turning the spigot and marking the spoon shape.

being drawn on. The reason for leaving the bulk of the handle in its original section is to provide a solid base, making for good control when bandsawing the spoon profile. If all the handle section is turned to a cylinder, the subsequent bandsawing would be difficult and dangerous. Fig 10.15 clearly shows this principle, and Fig 10.10 shows the profile up to this juncture.

The waste wood between the turned cylinder and the base of the spoon is now bandsawn away, leaving the profile shown in Fig 10.11.

The sawn blank can now be mounted in a chuck, as in Fig 10.16 (I used the Axminster four-jaw chuck with the 1in/25mm O'Donnell jaws – *see* page 5). The handle section can now be turned to a cylinder with a roughing gouge (*see* Figs 10.12, 10.13 and 10.17).

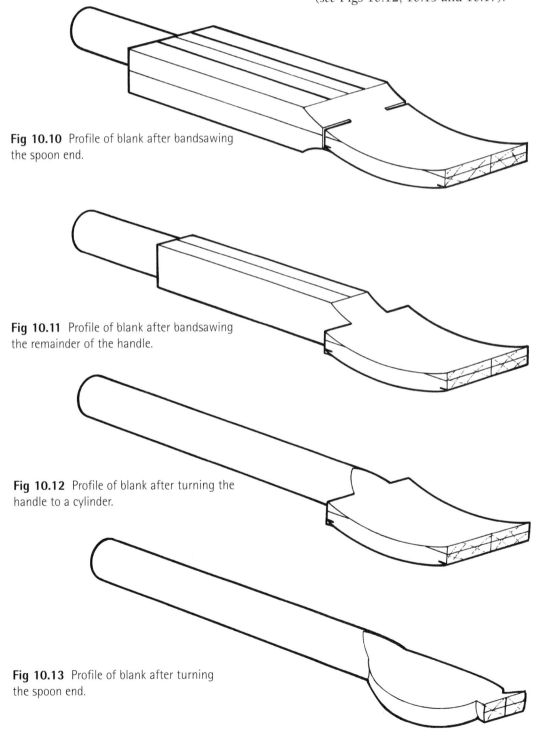

Fig 10.10 Profile of blank after bandsawing the spoon end.

Fig 10.11 Profile of blank after bandsawing the remainder of the handle.

Fig 10.12 Profile of blank after turning the handle to a cylinder.

Fig 10.13 Profile of blank after turning the spoon end.

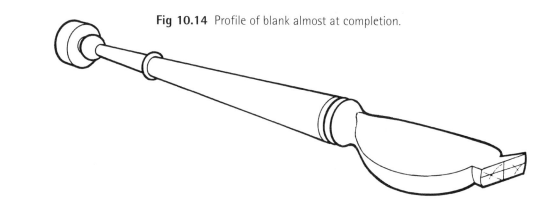

Fig 10.14 Profile of blank almost at completion.

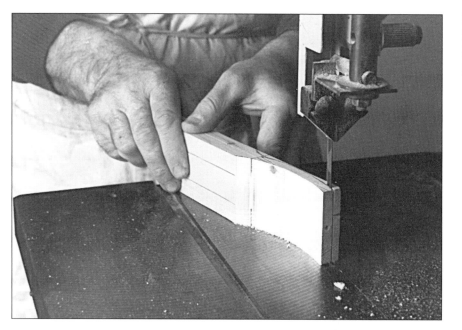

Fig 10.15 Bandsawing the spoon profile. Note how the flat section provides positive control.

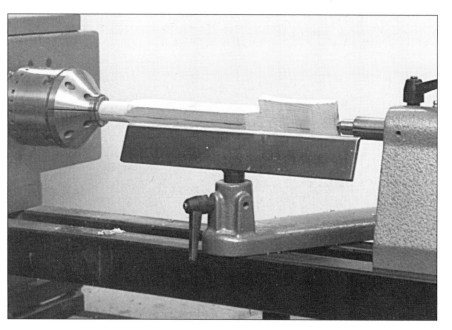

Fig 10.16 The bandsawn blank 'chucked up' and ready for turning.

Fig 10.17 Turning the handle to a cylinder with a roughing gouge.

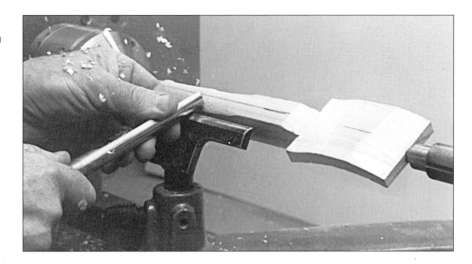

The same tool can be used for shaping part of the spoon end (*see* Fig 10.18), completing with a ³⁄₈in (10mm) spindle gouge, which is also used to form the cove, the V-cuts and the narrow flush bead where the handle and spoon merge (*see* Figs 10.19 and 10.20).

Fig 10.18 Initial shaping of the spoon with the roughing gouge.

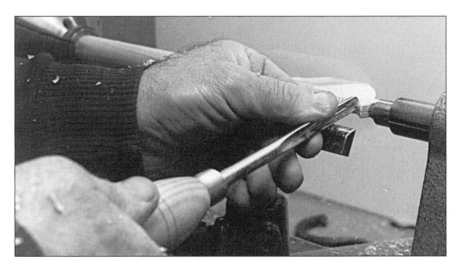

Fig 10.19 Refining the profile of the spoon end with a spindle gouge.

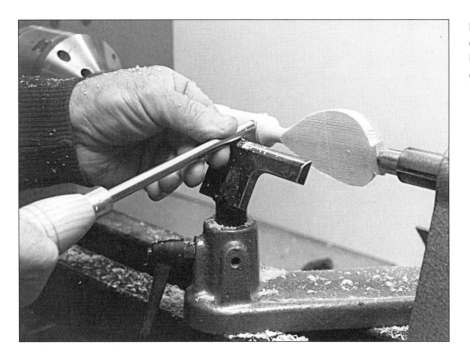

Fig 10.20 Forming the cove, V-cuts and flush bead with a spindle gouge.

The taper on the handle can be worked with a skew chisel (*see* Fig 10.21) traversing from left to right (downhill), remembering to allow for the raised bead near the end. The ball at the very end can be fashioned with the same tool or with a spindle gouge as shown in Fig 10.22.

Go through the sanding process, taking great care on the spoon profile as there is a lot of 'fresh air' sanding. I do not advise parting

right through at the spoon end (tailstock) – it is safer to leave a small area to be sawn off when removed from the lathe (*see* Fig 10.14).

It is safe to part off at the headstock end with this chucking system, as long as the server is cradled with the fingers of one hand when doing so.

Remove it from the lathe, trim off the waste at the spoon end and hand sand to blend it into

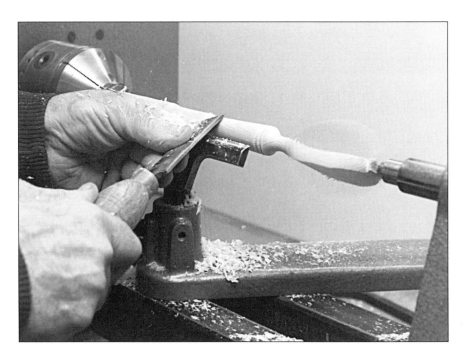

Fig 10.21 Forming the taper on the handle with a skew chisel.

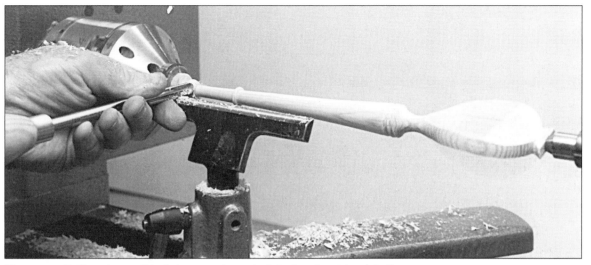

Fig 10.22 Rolling the small ball shape at the end of the handle with a spindle gouge.

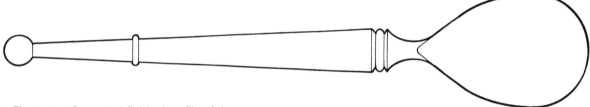

Fig 10.23 Suggested finished profile of the spoon.

the profile. To smooth off the sawn profiles on both sides of the spoon I make use of quick-change drum sanders (from Carrol Sanders Ltd, *see* page 162) which certainly speed up the operation and leave a super finish. The spoon should now resemble the outline shown in Fig 10.23.

Repeat the process for the second server. The one selected for the fork is completed by boring a ⅝in (16mm) hole and sawing to the dimensions shown in Fig 10.24. A few coats of oil completes the servers.

STAINLESS STEEL SERVERS

The servers I used in the example were obtained from Alan Holtham's The Old Stores Turnery, but similar servers can be obtained from other suppliers, for example Craft Supplies Ltd, or John Boddy's Fine Wood and Tool Store (*see* page 162). The making of the handles, as shown in the example (*see* Fig 10.25), is a straightforward spindle-turning exercise, with the same chucking system being employed.

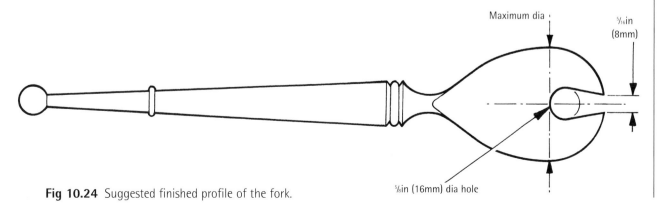

Fig 10.24 Suggested finished profile of the fork.

Maximum dia

⁵⁄₁₆in (8mm)

⅝in (16mm) dia hole

Cut the stock oversize to about 9in (229mm) long and 1in (25mm) square. A hole is required in one end to take the tang of the server on a tight fit. This can be drilled either on the lathe or on the pillar drill. Mount between centres (the hole at the tailstock end) and reduce it to a cylinder before re-chucking in the spigot chuck. Turn to the desired shape, sand and oil, and complete the project by gluing in the tang with something like Araldite.

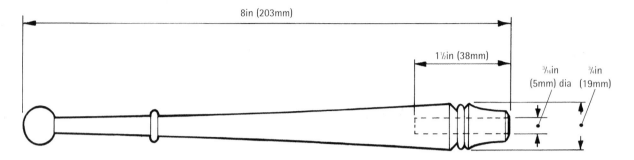

Fig 10.25 Profile and dimensional details of handle for stainless steel servers.

Light pulls (page 9)

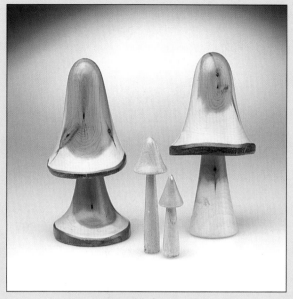

Toadstools (page 13)

Wooden eggs (page 18)

Cheeseboard with ceramic tile insert (page 25)

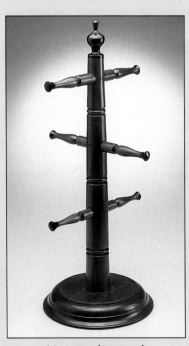

Earring stand (page 36)　　Mug tree (page 30)　　Finger-ring stand (page 42)

Salad bowl and servers (page 47)

Hourglass stand (page 57)

Novelty clock (page 66)

Bar stool (page 76)   Spinning stool (page 86)

Two-piece hollow form (page 94)

Gavel and anvil (page 100)

Egg cups and stand (page 115)

Birthday box (page108)

Pocket watch stand (page 131)

Square-edge bowls (page 123)

Pair of matching urns (page 140)

Goblets (page 149)

Chapter 11
Hourglass Stand

TIME: 4½ HOURS ★★★

Judging by the large number of outlets which advertise hourglasses, it would appear that making the required stand to accommodate them is a popular project for woodturners. The glasses are available in a variety of sizes to measure different timescales and with a choice of sand colour.

The one used in this example was obtained through Craft Supplies Ltd (*see* page 162), and is one of the larger ones advertised. It does, in fact, measure one hour, give or take a few seconds.

DESIGN CONSIDERATIONS

Objects holding fascination for children (which hourglasses certainly do) are inevitably touched and picked up. For this reason, it is not uncommon for them to get broken (and not only by children), and this influenced me to design a 'knock-down' stand, making use of Scan 50mm x M6 connecting bolts and matching brass heads. The normal method of gluing the joints together means that the whole unit is lost if the glass gets broken. With this design, the stand will easily come apart, enabling a new glass to be fitted. (The Scan fittings are available from Woodfit Ltd, *see* page 162). Fig 11.1 shows the completed stand.

Many stands are constructed with four uprights or spindles, but I have opted for three because the feet screwed to each (at both ends) provide greater stability when standing on uneven surfaces.

The shoulder length on the spindles needs to be calculated to suit the height of the particular glass. The glass in the example is 10⅜in (264mm), excluding the seals on each end: the shoulder lengths are ¹⁄₁₆in (1.5mm)

Fig 11.1 The completed project.

longer so that the ends do not tighten on to the glass. Similarly, the holes bored in the ends to take the spindles need to be positioned so that the spindles clear the glass.

Because the design of the ends incorporates a turned profile on both sides (adjacent to the edges), I opted to use the Craft Supplies Precision Combination Chuck with the parallel woodscrew chuck attachment for turning them. This enables reverse chucking to be undertaken without loss of true running.

The through hole bored to take the woodscrew chuck will not be seen when the project is completed. It is cloaked on the insides of the ends by the glass and by the decorative caps on the outside faces.

Careful study of Figs 11.2–11.8 is essential before commencing the project. Additionally, the photograph of the component parts, Fig 11.9 (clearly showing the connecting bolts and brass nuts), should assist greatly.

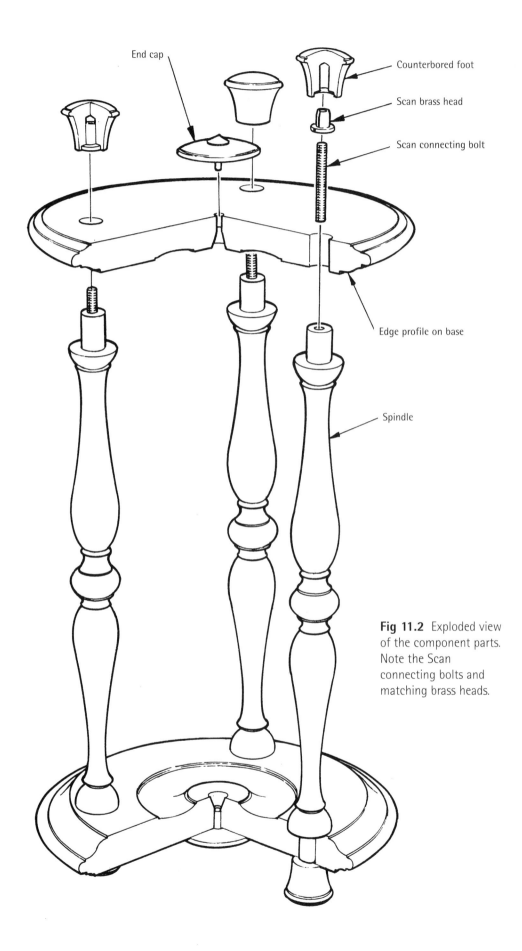

End cap

Counterbored foot

Scan brass head

Scan connecting bolt

Edge profile on base

Spindle

Fig 11.2 Exploded view of the component parts. Note the Scan connecting bolts and matching brass heads.

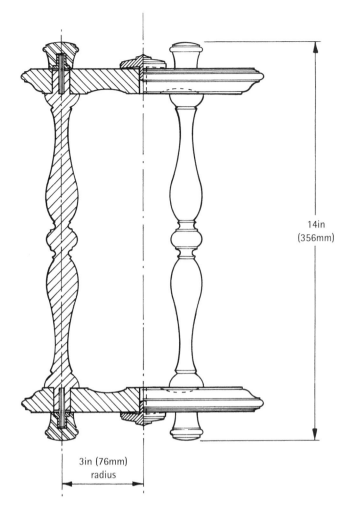

Fig 11.3 Dimensional details and section through the stand.

Fig 11.4 (below left) Plan view of outside of main disc, showing the through holes for the spindles and the screw chuck.

Fig 11.5 (below right) Plan view of inside of main disc, together with elevation and section through.

14in (356mm)

3in (76mm) radius

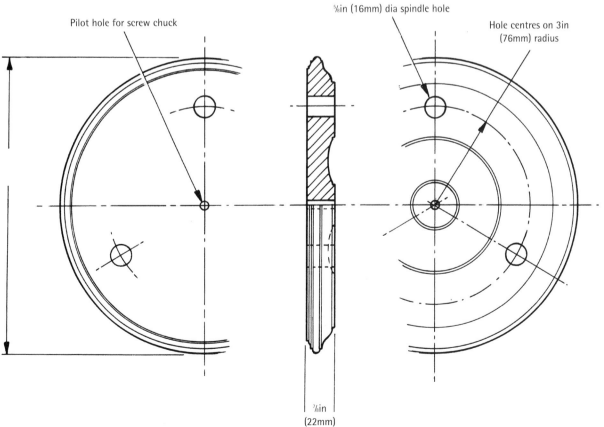

Pilot hole for screw chuck

⅝in (16mm) dia spindle hole

Hole centres on 3in (76mm) radius

⅞in (22mm)

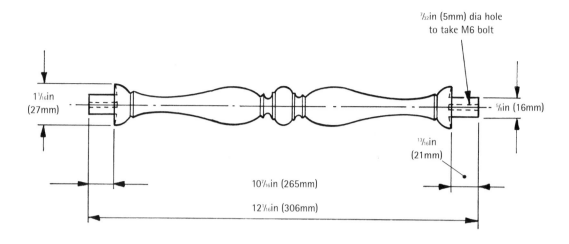

7/32in (5mm) dia hole
to take M6 bolt

1 1/16in
(27mm)

5/8in (16mm)

13/16in
(21mm)

10 7/16in (265mm)

12 1/16in (306mm)

Fig 11.6 (above)
Dimensional details of a
spindle. Note the 7/32in
(5mm) hole bored in
each end to take the
connecting bolt and also
how the spigot shoulders
have been slightly
undercut to ensure a
flush fit with the ends.

Fig 11.7 (right)
Dimensional details of
the feet. Note the
counterbore to allow the
brass heads to finish
flush to the surface.

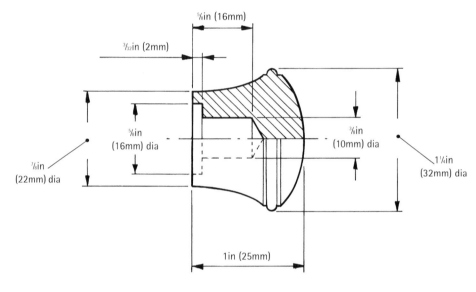

5/8in (16mm)

3/32in (2mm)

5/8in
(16mm) dia

3/8in
(10mm) dia

7/8in
(22mm) dia

1 1/4in
(32mm) dia

1in (25mm)

Fig 11.8 Dimensional
details of the end caps.
Note that the shoulders
have again been slightly
undercut.

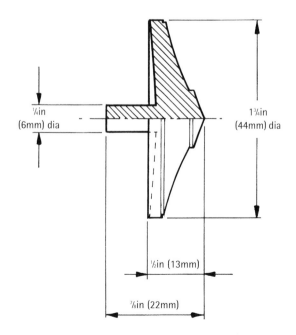

1/4in
(6mm) dia

1 3/4in
(44mm) dia

1/2in (13mm)

7/8in (22mm)

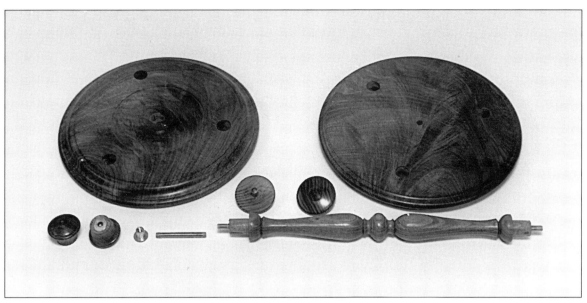

Fig 11.9 The component parts and fittings.

CHOICE AND PREPARATION OF STOCK

Walnut was my choice for this project, influenced by the fact that it is renowned for its dimensional stability and general appeal. Your choice can be different, but species prone to warping should not be considered. I have heard it argued that the ends should be re-sawn from stock of 'double thickness', that is to say, where two 1in (25mm) thick pieces are required (as in this case) a 2in (51mm) thick board is sawn down the middle. This, of course, will ensure a perfect grain match.

I do not, however, go along with this at all. In the first place, very few woodturners have access to a machine capable of re-sawing 9in x 2in (229mm x 51mm) stock. Secondly, no matter how dry and stable the wood, the process of re-sawing will in all probability lead to warping. I therefore choose 1in (25mm) thick stock for the ends, although I match up the grain and colour as well as I am able.

Ideally, the board used for the ends should be planed true and to a constant thickness of a full $^7\!/\!_8$in (22mm). A 9in (229mm) circular template can be made to scribe the outer perimeter, to prick mark dead centre and also the hole centres for the spindles.

The three spindles are cut from $1^1\!/\!_4$in (32mm) stock, to the finished length of $12^1\!/\!_{16}$in (307mm). The six feet should be cut to approximately $1^1\!/\!_2$in (38mm) cubes, and the two end caps from 2in (51mm) square stock to a length of approximately $1^1\!/\!_2$in (38mm).

ORDER OF WORK

ENDS

These are best drilled on a pillar drill, but alternative methods have been discussed previously. In the interests of accuracy, it is advisable to bore both pieces together. By referring to Fig 11.10 (please note that MDF has been used in the photograph for convenience) it will be seen that both have been securely clamped to the pillar drill table before boring the first $^5\!/\!_8$in (16mm) diameter hole. A couple of strips of double-sided tape sandwiched between the two will prevent any movement.

Note also how the grain direction has been lined up and the holes numbered and dead-centre marked (the ends must subsequently be assembled in the position as drilled).

After the three spindle holes have been bored, a $^1\!/\!_4$in (6mm) hole is drilled dead centre to accommodate the screw chuck. Continue by bandsawing to shape, and then mount on the screw chuck with the intended 'inside' in view. Run the lathe at approximately 1000rpm and

61

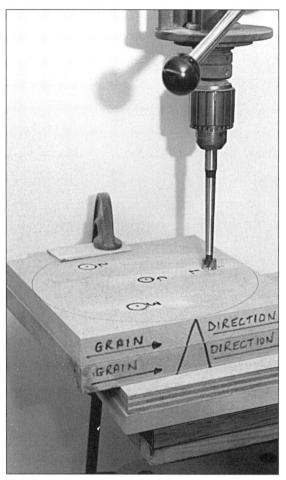

Fig 11.10 Method of boring the two ends together. Note how securely they are clamped, and how the grain direction has been lined up.

pencil in the 1¼in (32mm) diameter flat area near the centre, and also the extent of the hollow on a 2in (51mm) radius.

Fig 11.11 should make the process clear. The hollow has been formed with a gouge and round-nose scraper, and a spindle gouge is being used to fashion the desired profile near the edge. At this stage a small hollow needs to be formed at the centre to take the end seal on the glass. Now go through the sanding sequence to about 320 grit.

The end can now be reverse chucked, allowing the top to be cleaned up and the edge profile completed with gouge and scrapers. Now sand and repeat the process on the other blank.

SPINDLES

Having cut the three to the required length of 12¹⁄₁₆in (307mm), a ⁷⁄₃₂in (5mm) hole is required in the dead centre of both ends to take the M6 threaded rod. This can be done on the lathe as described previously, but I prefer to use the pillar drill.

The square section is gripped in a vice and lined up with the central pillar of the drill to ensure accurate, vertical boring (*see* Fig 11.12). Drill to a depth of about 1in (25mm) and then complete the other five holes in identical fashion.

Fig 11.11 The inside of an end being profiled with a ³⁄₈in (10mm) spindle gouge, held well on its side and being pulled from small to large diameter. The large hollow was formed with the same tool followed by refinement with a round-nose scraper.

Fig 11.12 Method of boring the ends of the spindle blanks to take the connecting rods. Note the secure clamping arrangement, the wood having been lined up in the vertical plane by sighting through on the pillar of the drill press.

To provide for ease of screwing the 2in (51mm) lengths of threaded rod into the holes, I secured the rod in a wooden-jawed vice and turned the still square-section wood by hand until the required depth was reached (the rod is subsequently glued in with Araldite to prevent it spinning).

Repeat the process with the other five holes, but the rods must obviously be removed for the subsequent turning.

To drive the spindle between centres it is now necessary to make use of a scrapwood spigot (fixed to a screw chuck) which, when combined with the compression applied by the tailstock, will be adequate.

Reduce the stock to a cylinder and to the required diameter. The spindles are a copy turning exercise, so use can be made of a marking stick to mark on the salient points. Fig 11.13 shows the marking stick in use, and the scrapwood spigot can also be seen clearly. Note from the photograph that only one-half of the marking stick is set out with the profile and sizing positions. This is because the pattern is repeated either side of the central bead, and accurate setting out is more easily achieved by turning the stick end-to-end and registering on the centre marks of wood and stick.

After sizing in to the required diameters at the appropriate marks, the profiles are worked

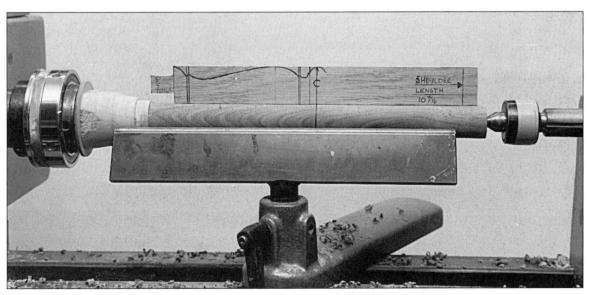

Fig 11.13 Marking stick in use to transfer the salient profile points to the spindle blank. Note that, for accurate marking, the stick is turned end-to-end and registered on the centre marks.

with gouges and chisels. Fig 11.14 shows a ½in (13mm) skew chisel being used to refine the profile near the centre of the spindle. Note also the left hand cradling the stock to prevent vibration.

Sand each spindle carefully, taking care not to destroy the crispness of your turning. After completing all three, test the fit of each spigot and trim if required. An overtight fit is not necessary.

FEET

By referring to Figs 11.2 and 11.7 it will be seen that the brass heads are counterbored (⅝in/16mm diameter x 3/32in/2mm deep) to enable the heads to finish flush with the surface of the wood. I do this on the pillar drill, boring all six feet before changing to a ⅜in (10mm)

drill bit to deepen each hole (to a depth of ¾in/19mm) to receive the body of the brass heads.

Again I make use of a scrapwood spigot to drive the feet. The tailstock can be used to provide support while the bulk of the profiling with gouge and chisel is done. For the refining cuts at the very end the tailstock is obviously removed, and Fig 11.15 shows a ½in (13mm) skew chisel being used for this purpose. Sand and polish as required, and repeat the process five more times.

END CAPS

The prepared blanks are mounted on the screw chuck and brought to the largest required diameter of 1¾in (44mm). The profile can now be set out, marking in the length of the spigot

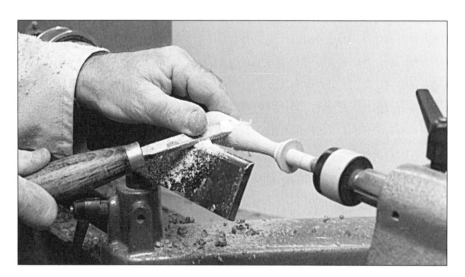

Fig 11.14 A spindle being refined with a ½in (13mm) skew chisel. Note that the cutting is 'downhill', and also that the left hand is cradling the work to prevent vibration.

Fig 11.15 The ½in (13mm) skew again being employed to refine the top of one of the feet. Note that the foot is being driven on a scrapwood spigot.

($^3/_8$in/10mm) and the overall length of $^7/_8$in (22mm). It is important to complete the profiling on the top of the cap before cutting the $^1/_4$in (6mm) diameter spigot, or vibration will almost certainly ensue. Sand and polish as before, but before parting off. Make sure that the shoulders on the joint are slightly undercut so as to ensure a flush fit on the ends (*see* Fig 11.8).

ASSEMBLY

The connecting bolts are cut to the appropriate length and secured in the ends of the spindles with Araldite or some similar adhesive. The brass heads are secured to the feet in a similar manner. Before gluing in the brass heads, the holes at the $^5/_8$in (16mm) diameter ends must be drilled out to enable the connecting bolt to pass through them. (The fitting is designed to operate the other way round, but of course that wouldn't work in this mode of use.)

It is *vital* that sufficient time is allowed for the glue to cure before attempting to screw the components together. I suggest that they be left overnight.

Final assembly is now a straightforward and simple task, as is the 'knock-down' process if required. I do not find it necessary to glue in the two decorative end caps, as I am careful to form a good push fit joint.

FINISHING

Many will opt to apply their choice of finish such as sealing and waxing, friction polish, etc., on the lathe. My choice is to apply one coat of sealer and de-nib each component on the lathe, followed by the application of two spray coats of a tough melamine-based lacquer.

By this time you will have earned an hour's relaxation, and what better way to relax than sit and watch the sand pass from the top half to the bottom half of the glass!

Chapter 12
Novelty Clock

TIME: 3¾ HOURS ★★★

Clock movements of all shapes and sizes are readily available from many sources. They are also comparatively inexpensive, and the quartz movements are extremely reliable.

I am afraid that I do not find many of the clocks that you see at craft fairs very appealing. The majority of the designs are dominated by either a tile or bezel, with the wood seemingly just something to fix it to.

DESIGN CONSIDERATIONS

I therefore wanted something where the turning part of the project offered more of a challenge than mounting a blank on a faceplate, making a hole for the movement and simply profiling the edges.

My design is based upon that of Mike Cripps, who makes similar stands for pressed flower arrangements. I have modified Mike's idea to suit a clock insert, the design being loosely translated from a Victorian pole screen.

I should have preferred a smaller and narrower clock insert, but the one in the example is the nearest size to what I wanted to satisfy my conception of proportion in this particular design. I feel that it may appear top-heavy viewed from the side, but I hope that I have sown the seeds for you to modify it if you want to. (This particular movement was obtained through Christopher Milner Fine Woodcraft, see page 162.)

Fig 12.1 shows the completed project. By studying the drawings in Figs 12.2 and 12.3 it will be seen that the main body is slotted out at the bottom to receive the tripod legs. Both ends of this component are also bored with a ⁵⁄₁₆in (8mm) hole to receive the lower finial and the parallel spindle respectively. The upper finial is bored with a ⁵⁄₁₆in (8mm) hole to allow for a push fit on to the top of the parallel spindle.

Fig 12.1 The completed project.

The clock surround is secured by two draught pieces, glued into the back of the surround, each bored to enable the spindle to pass through. The surround can then be moved up and down on the spindle to suit.

CHOICE AND PREPARATION OF STOCK

This particular example is in walnut, but yew wood is a favourite for this project. Any attractive hardwood is, of course, suitable, although the coarser-grained species should be avoided.

The clock surround is prepared from ¾in (19mm) thick stock. I used a plywood template (4in/102mm diameter) to prick both dead centre and the hole centres for the draughts (on

Fig 12.2 Exploded view of component parts.

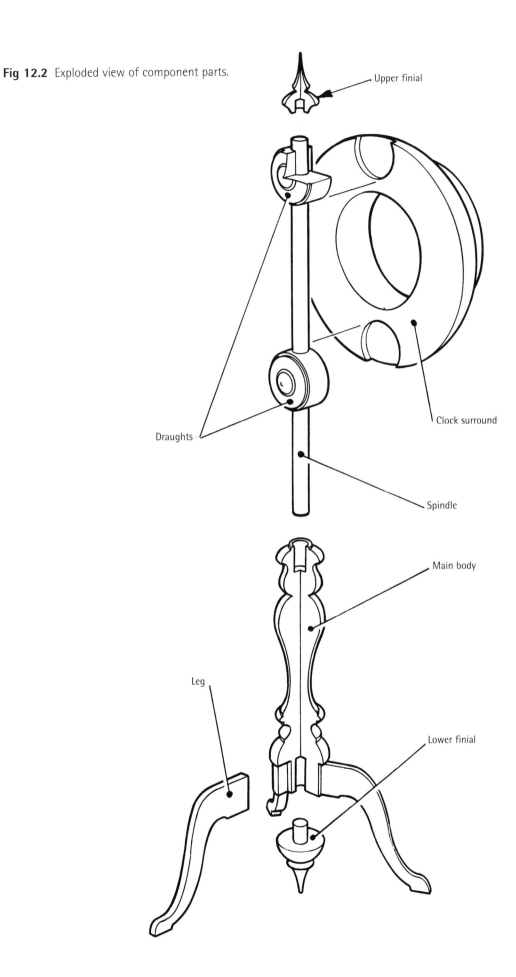

Upper finial

Clock surround

Draughts

Spindle

Main body

Leg

Lower finial

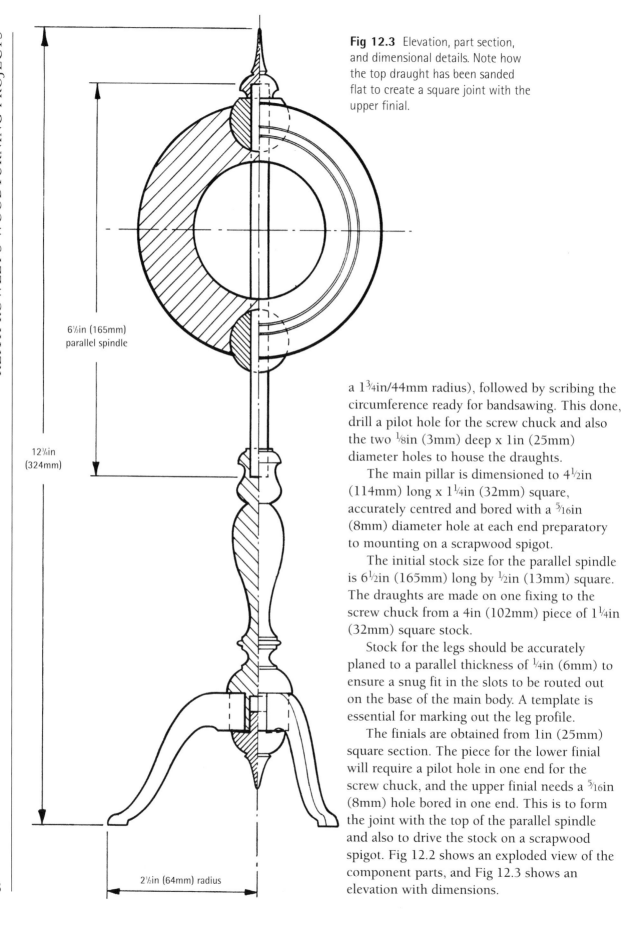

Fig 12.3 Elevation, part section, and dimensional details. Note how the top draught has been sanded flat to create a square joint with the upper finial.

6½in (165mm) parallel spindle

12¾in (324mm)

2½in (64mm) radius

a 1¾in/44mm radius), followed by scribing the circumference ready for bandsawing. This done, drill a pilot hole for the screw chuck and also the two ⅛in (3mm) deep x 1in (25mm) diameter holes to house the draughts.

The main pillar is dimensioned to 4½in (114mm) long x 1¼in (32mm) square, accurately centred and bored with a ⁵⁄₁₆in (8mm) diameter hole at each end preparatory to mounting on a scrapwood spigot.

The initial stock size for the parallel spindle is 6½in (165mm) long by ½in (13mm) square. The draughts are made on one fixing to the screw chuck from a 4in (102mm) piece of 1¼in (32mm) square stock.

Stock for the legs should be accurately planed to a parallel thickness of ¼in (6mm) to ensure a snug fit in the slots to be routed out on the base of the main body. A template is essential for marking out the leg profile.

The finials are obtained from 1in (25mm) square section. The piece for the lower finial will require a pilot hole in one end for the screw chuck, and the upper finial needs a ⁵⁄₁₆in (8mm) hole bored in one end. This is to form the joint with the top of the parallel spindle and also to drive the stock on a scrapwood spigot. Fig 12.2 shows an exploded view of the component parts, and Fig 12.3 shows an elevation with dimensions.

ORDER OF WORK

CLOCK SURROUND

Figs 12.4a and 12.4b provide dimensional
details of the surround. Note that 3½in
(89mm) hole centres for the two draughts
allow them to protrude beyond the
circumference of the surround. This actually
happened by mistake on the prototype, but I
thought that it looked better, so I now make
them all like that!

The sequence of chucking the blank is
shown in Figs 12.5a, b and c. The screw chuck
is employed throughout, with the intended
back of the surround pulled on to the face of
the chuck for the initial fixing. With a pair of
dividers, scribe a diameter of 2¼in (56mm) –
the body of the clock movement being 2⅛in
(55mm). With a parting tool and spindle
gouge, cut in to a depth of approximately ¼in
(6mm) (*see* Fig 12.5a).

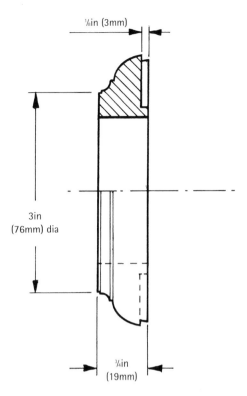

⅛in (3mm)

3in
(76mm) dia

¾in
(19mm)

Fig 12.4b End elevation
and dimensional details
of the clock surround.

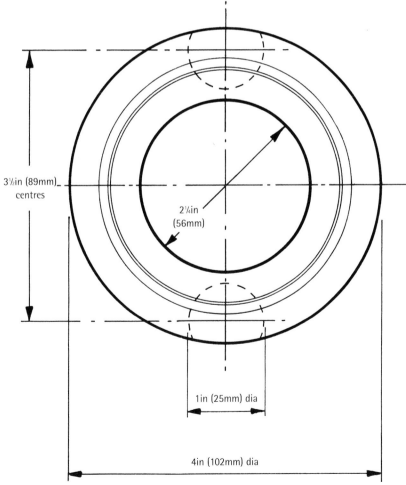

3½in (89mm)
centres

2¼in
(56mm)

1in (25mm) dia

4in (102mm) dia

Fig 12.4a Front
elevation and
dimensional details of
the clock surround.

69

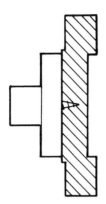

Fig 12.5a The surround has been mounted on the screw chuck, and the 2¼in (56mm) diameter x ¼in (6mm) deep recess has been formed with a gouge and parting tool. Note the two 1in (25mm) holes on the back to house the draughts.

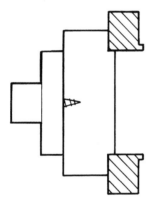

Fig 12.5b The surround has been reverse chucked on to a piece of scrapwood and the parting through completed.

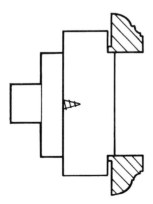

Fig 12.5c After reverse chucking again, the edge profile has been achieved with a gouge and parting tool.

A piece of scrapwood is now fixed to the screw chuck and a 2¼in (56mm) shoulder formed with a parting tool to take (on a push fit) the recess just cut. Now comes the parting-through process, which some turners find alarming. Be assured that there is no danger whatsoever if the tool rest is positioned as close as possible to the face of the wood and slightly above centre. Fig 12.5b shows the section after parting through.

After the waste piece is removed, the sides of the through hole can be squared up with a skew chisel used scraper fashion. Before removing the stock from this fixing, the back can be sanded and polished, but beware the two 1in (25mm) diameter blind holes (bored previously to house the draughts) – it is easy to get a nasty rap on the ends of your fingers. Remove the surround from the chuck and check that the movement fits. A tight fit is not advisable.

The surround is reverse chucked again by the same method and the profiling on the front edge can be worked. A spindle gouge will cope with most of the profiling, but it may be necessary to use a parting tool or square-ended scraper to form the two flat areas (fillets) (*see* Fig 12.5c).

Complete the surround by sanding and polishing.

MAIN BODY

The ⁵⁄₁₆in (8mm) holes in both ends means that a scrapwood spigot is required to drive the stock. After reducing the square to a cylinder of 1⅛in (28mm) diameter, the flat area 1in (25mm) diameter x ⁹⁄₁₆in (14mm) long (where the three leg slots are located) is formed. Note the shoulder which serves to cloak the top of the slots when the legs are subsequently fitted (*see* Figs 12.6a and 12.6b).

Before proceeding further it is advisable to router out these slots. This can be done by making use of the home-made device described in Chapter 5. I use a metal carrier which is made by Techlink Enterprises (*see* page 162), which is much more versatile and robust than the home-made wooden version.

Fig 12.7 shows the carrier in use, supported on an MDF platform secured to the bed bars. Note that the router can easily be moved up

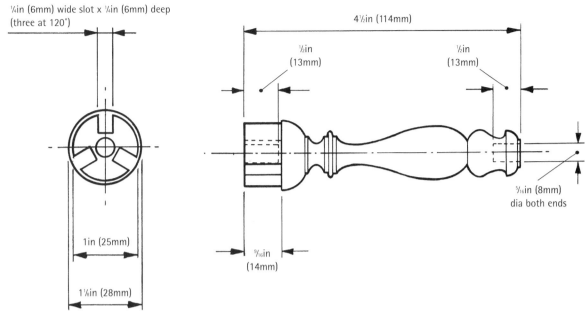

¼in (6mm) wide slot x ¼in (6mm) deep
(three at 120°)

4½in (114mm)

½in
(13mm)

½in
(13mm)

⁵⁄₁₆in (8mm)
dia both ends

1in (25mm)

1⅛in (28mm)

⁹⁄₁₆in
(14mm)

Fig 12.6a End elevation of main body showing how the slots are set out and dimensional details.

Fig 12.6b Profile and dimensional details of the main body.

and down in the slotted frame to suit the height of the lathe centres. The depth of the cut, as can be seen in the photograph, is set by clamping a piece of wood on the back of the platform.

The dividing head will have to be used to locate the three slots at 120° intervals, and each slot will need squaring out at the shoulder end.

Fig 12.8 shows this being done with a ¼in (6mm) bevel-edged chisel.

The cylinder can now be turned to the profile shown in Fig 12.6b, and the 'detail gouge' is capable of completing most of it, with just a little help from a parting tool to square off the fillets. Sand and polish as required. Fig 12.9 shows the 'detail gouge' in use.

Fig 12.7 The metal router carrier being used to slot out the leg housings. Note the piece of wood clamped to the MDF platform to regulate the depth of cut.

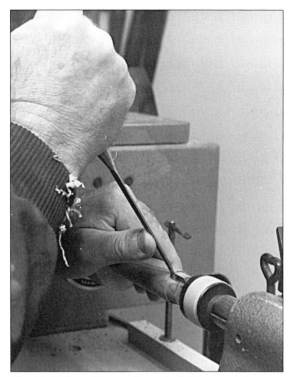

Fig 12.8 Squaring out the end of the routed slots with a ¼in (6mm) bevel-edged chisel.

Fig 12.9 The 'detail gouge' being used to refine the shape of the main body. Note the scrapwood chuck driving the stock.

PARALLEL SPINDLE

This is a fairly simple component to make. Mount between centres and apply only minimum pressure on the tailstock (to prevent splitting the wood), rough down and plane off with a skew chisel. Calipers should be used to obtain an accurate parallel cylinder. Lightly sand and polish.

DRAUGHTS

So named because they look like them and I couldn't think of anything better to call them. Mount the stock on the screw chuck and turn to a cylinder (leave it oversize until after the drilling operation – any 'break-out' will then be turned away). Follow this by setting out the position of both of the draughts with the aid of

Fig 12.10 Elevations of a draught, together with dimensional details.

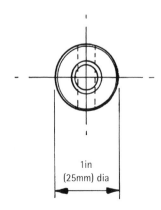

1in
(25mm) dia

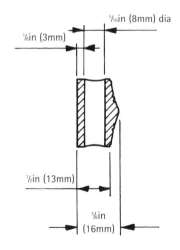

⁵⁄₁₆in (8mm) dia

⅛in (3mm)

½in (13mm)

⅝in
(16mm)

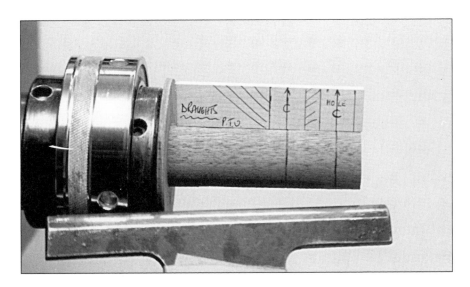

Fig 12.11 The stock for the draughts has been mounted on a screw chuck and the hole centres marked with the aid of the template.

a template. Fig 12.10 shows dimensional details, and Fig 12.11 shows the template offered up to the wood with the hole centres marked.

A drilling jig is helpful to ensure accurate radial drilling of the two $^5/_{16}$in (8mm) holes. Fig 12.12 shows such a device which is nothing more than a length of 1$^1/_2$in (38mm) square stock with a cylinder turned on one end to fit in the tool post. The square shoulder registers in the same place every time it is used.

To find centre height on the jig, locate it in the toolpost and bring up the tailstock, and allow the revolving centre to make a slight mark on the wood. Now bore the hole in the

Fig 12.12 Simple drilling jig which locates in the toolpost; the square section will register to the same depth every time.

Fig 12.13 Boring the holes in the draughts. Exact centre height on the jig has been marked with a live centre in the tailstock.

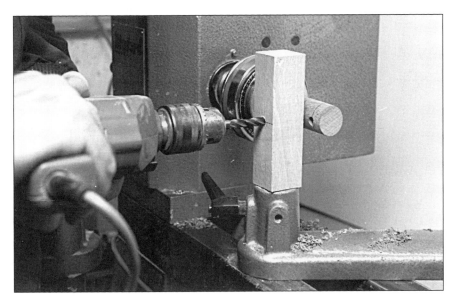

Fig 12.14 The first draught being parted off.

jig and continue by setting it up in the required positions to bore the holes in the draughts (make sure the dividing head is engaged). Fig 12.13 shows the jig in use.

With both holes bored, the stock can be reduced to 1in (25mm) diameter to give a good push fit in the corresponding holes on the surround. Profile as shown in the drawings, and part off after sanding and polishing. Fig 12.14 shows the first draught being parted off. Note that a section of the upper draught is sanded flat to provide for a square joint with the upper finial (see Fig 12.3).

LEGS

To ensure that all three legs are identical I suggest that three pieces of the ¼in (6mm) thick stock are stuck together with double-sided tape. The profile can then be marked on with a previously made template. It is important that the grain is aligned to provide maximum strength (see Fig 12.15).

I use a Hegner power fret saw to cut the legs, but it is possible to cut them with hand-held tools such as a coping saw. A light sanding is necessary to smooth off the edges.

LOWER FINIAL

The 1in (25mm) square-section stock is mounted on the screw chuck and turned to the profile shown in Fig 12.16. The ⁵⁄₁₆in (8mm)

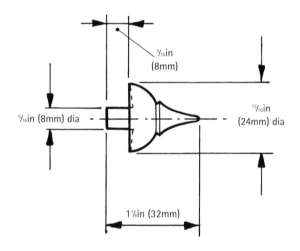

Fig 12.16 Profile and dimensional details – lower finial.

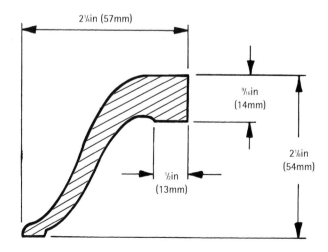

Fig 12.15 Profile and dimensional details of the legs. Note how the grain has been aligned to provide maximum strength.

spigot needs to be a good push fit in the corresponding hole at the base of the main body.

UPPER FINIAL

The stock will need a $^5/_{16}$in (8mm) hole bored in one end to fit on to the top of the parallel spindle. This will also enable a scrapwood spigot to be used to drive it while being turned (*see* Fig 12.17).

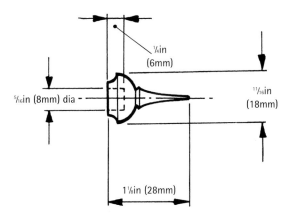

Fig 12.17 Profile and dimensional details – upper finial.

ASSEMBLY

After a 'dry' assembly to ensure that all the components fit together satisfactorily, start by gluing in the three legs. To prevent any tilt on the project, it is vital that the three legs lie exactly in the same plane. This is easily achieved by mounting the assembly on the lathe, positioning the tool rest so that the very tip of one leg brushes it and then adjusting the other two in the same manner.

PVA glue is used for all the joints with the exception of the draughts. For these I use superglue which provides for almost instant and permanent positioning. It is obviously most important that the holes in the draughts are lined up before the glue grabs, and to ensure this the parallel spindle can be used as shown in Fig 12.2.

FINISHING

You may well decide to polish each component on the lathe; the legs will require polishing separately, of course. I apply three coats of sprayed lacquer, which gives an excellent finish.

Chapter 13
Bar Stool

TIME: 5 HOURS ★ ★ ★

These are becoming increasingly popular as more and more people refurbish or create 'live in' kitchens. Unfortunately, many of the stools I see in the shops are of dubious quality, flimsy in design and rarely produced other than in substandard pine. There is, however, nothing wrong with pine, this species being the choice of many for kitchen units, and I have made a good many stools in good-quality, clean and straight-grained Scots pine.

Probably the most favoured wood for kitchen fittings is oak and, as I was fortunate enough to acquire some short ends of my favourite English variety, I took the opportunity of using some for this particular project.

This is a fairly simple exercise combining faceplate and spindle turning. It also provides a test of repetition turning skills in producing the four 'identical' legs.

DESIGN CONSIDERATIONS

This example (*see* Fig 13.1) was copied from a stool I bought for a song from a car boot sale, and it would be difficult to design anything more traditional. It is sturdy without looking too heavy and clumsy.

For stability, the four legs are splayed so that the bottom of each is outside the line of a perpendicular projected from the edge of the seat. For comfort, the edges of the seat are well rounded over and the top is also slightly dished.

The height of the stool can be made to suit: what might be comfortable for a tall person will not be ideal for a person much shorter in stature. The measurements given in the illustrations for this project are only a guide, and can be adjusted according to personal preference.

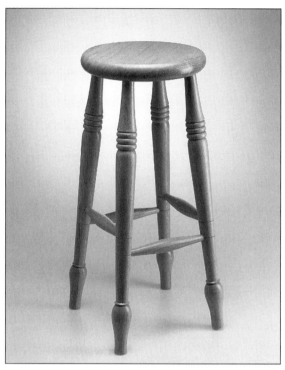

Fig 13.1 The completed project.

CHOICE AND PREPARATION OF STOCK

In addition to pine and oak, ash, elm and beech are also eminently suitable. Ideally, the top should be in one piece and 'quarter sawn' to minimize warping. This may not always be possible, however, and there is nothing wrong with edge jointing two or three narrower boards.

The timber for the legs and stretchers should be chosen with great care, as it is essential that clean, straight-grained pieces are used. The piece of timber for the top should have one side planed to a smooth finish (the intended underside). If possible, all the component parts should be cut from the same board to give a good grain and colour match.

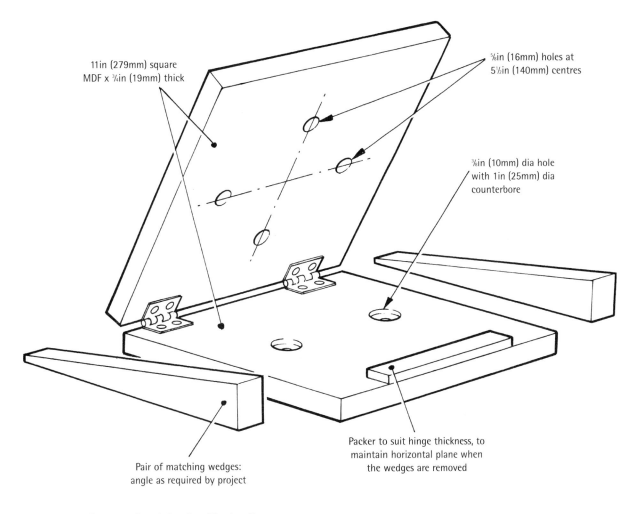

11in (279mm) square
MDF x ¾in (19mm) thick

⅝in (16mm) holes at
5½in (140mm) centres

⅜in (10mm) dia hole
with 1in (25mm) dia
counterbore

Pair of matching wedges:
angle as required by project

Packer to suit hinge thickness, to
maintain horizontal plane when
the wedges are removed

Fig 13.2 Constructional details of boring jig.

ORDER OF WORK

The underside of the seat is marked out with
diagonal lines, and from their intersection an
11¾in (298mm) circle is struck with dividers.
The positions of the four holes are then marked
in on the diagonal lines at a distance of 4⅜in
(112mm) from the centre. All four marks are
best reinforced with a pointed awl to ensure
positive location for the drill bit. A pilot hole to
accommodate the woodscrew chuck is also
required on the dead-centre mark, and then the
stock can be brought to a circle on the
bandsaw.

BORING THE SEAT HOLES

There are several methods of doing this and
probably the easiest and best is to make use of a
pillar drill. A jig is required to simplify the
process, and also to bore the holes in the legs to
receive the stretchers. (The jig will prove
invaluable for many similar applications,
including other projects later in this book.)

Fig 13.2 provides constructional details of
such a jig. It is nothing more than two pieces of
MDF hinged together, with the lower section
drilled and counter-bored to enable it to be
bolted to the pillar drill table with no part of
the bolt heads protruding. This type of jig
allows for the insertion of a pair of matching
wedges positioned at opposite ends, the angle of
the wedges being cut to an appropriate angle.

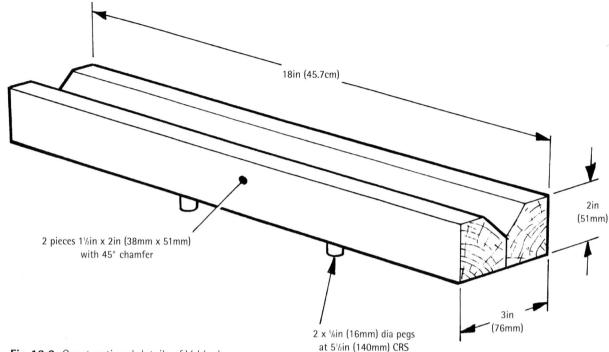

18in (45.7cm)

2 pieces 1½in x 2in (38mm x 51mm)
with 45° chamfer

2 x ⅝in (16mm) dia pegs
at 5½in (140mm) CRS

2in
(51mm)

3in
(76mm)

Fig 13.3 Constructional details of V-block.

The uppermost table is also bored with two sets of holes at right angles and at 5½in (140mm) centres. These will accommodate the ⅝in (16mm) diameter pegs on the underside of the V-block in which the legs (or any round stock) are cradled while being bored.

The V-block, shown in Fig 13.3, is simply two pieces of 1½in x 2in (38mm x 51mm), with a 45° chamfer worked on each piece, glued and screwed together and with two pieces of ⅝in (16mm) dowel sunk in the underside to fit in the corresponding holes in the top platform.

By referring to the half-elevations shown in Fig 13.4, it will be seen that the angle of the wedges for drilling the seat is 7° and the angle for the stretchers is 5°. These can now be set out using a protractor and adjustable bevel and cut to size on the bandsaw.

In the interests of safety, the seat should be securely clamped to the jig while boring the ⅞in (22mm) diameter holes. I use a sawtooth bit, making sure that the depth stop on the pillar drill is correctly adjusted to prevent boring the holes too deep. To ensure accurate drilling, the diagonal pencil lines on the underside of the seat must be lined up with the

centre of the pillar, as shown in Fig 13.5. (Please note that the clamps have been removed in the photograph for clarity.)

With the four holes bored, the blank can now be mounted on the screw chuck and, with the lathe running at about 1000rpm, both the face and edge can be brought into balance with a ⅜in (10mm) bowl gouge turned well over on its side. This will ensure that only the supported tool edge will be in contact with the whirling wood, thus avoiding any tendency to dig in.

The radius on the edge is formed with the same tool, again used well over on its side and pulled towards you, that is, from small to large diameter, which means cutting with the grain (*see* Fig 13.6). The radius can be refined with a square-ended scraper if necessary.

The slight dishing on the seat top is easily achieved with the bowl gouge, followed by refining cuts with a domed scraper. Complete the seat by sanding down to about 320 grit paper.

Fig 13.4 Half-elevations showing method of determining true angles of legs and stretchers.

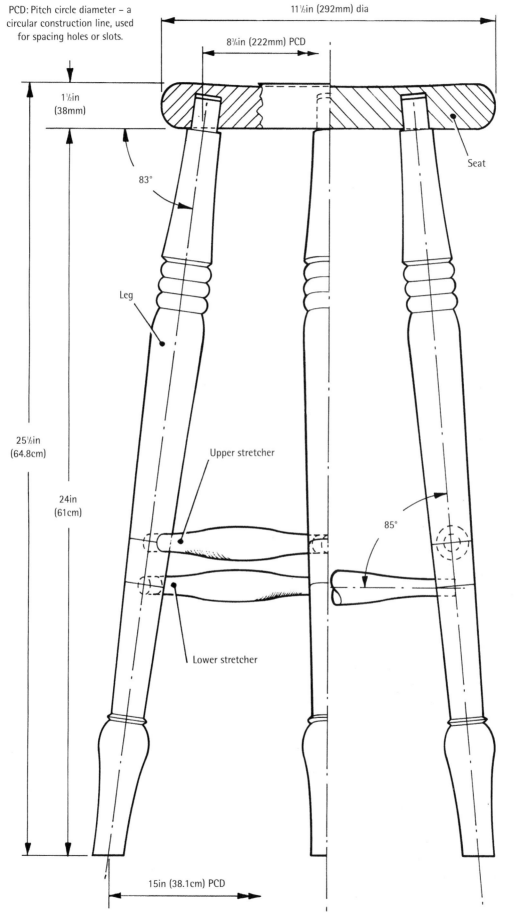

PCD: Pitch circle diameter – a circular construction line, used for spacing holes or slots.

11½in (292mm) dia

8¾in (222mm) PCD

1½in (38mm)

83°

Seat

Leg

25½in (64.8cm)

24in (61cm)

Upper stretcher

85°

Lower stretcher

15in (38.1cm) PCD

Half-elevation showing true angle of leg

Half-elevation (stool turned through 45°) showing the relationship of stretcher to leg

79

Fig 13.5 Boring jig in use for the seat holes. The tapered 7° wedges can be clearly seen, as can the method of lining up the pencil marks with the central pillar of the drill press.

Fig 13.6 Rounding over the seat edges. Note that the gouge is well over on its side (flute facing the direction of cut) and being pulled from small to large diameter.

Fig 13.7 Dimensional details of leg and stretcher hole centres from which a marking stick or rod can be made.

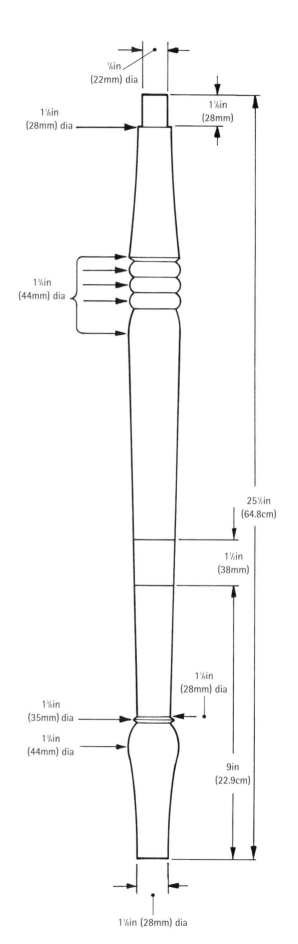

⅞in (22mm) dia

1⅛in (28mm) dia

1⅛in (28mm)

1¾in (44mm) dia

25½in (64.8cm)

1½in (38mm)

1⅛in (28mm) dia

1⅜in (35mm) dia

1¾in (44mm) dia

9in (22.9cm)

1⅛in (28mm) dia

LEGS

These are prepared from 2in (51mm) stock and cut to their finished length. Careful study of Fig 13.7 will assist in the preparation of a full-size marking stick or rod. These are invaluable in repetition turning, and all the salient profile points and various diameters can be marked on them. The rod can be made from thick card, plywood or thin-section wood.

There are four main diameters to size to on this particular design, and if you possess only one set of calipers you may well wish to make a sizing stick as shown in Fig 13.8. This can be a piece of scrap wood turned down to a tapered cylinder with shallow chisel nicks on the appropriate diameters. Using a sizing stick is much quicker and more accurate than using a ruler.

I have several sets of calipers, and my method is to permanently mark the four diameters on the rod and colour code them to identical coloured tape stuck to the calipers. This provides for very quick setting-up, and also avoids using the wrong set to size in.

Mount the first leg between centres (about 2000rpm) and reduce the stock to a parallel cylinder, making use of the caliper set at 1¾in (44mm) to arrive at the thickest diameter. Move the tool rest close to the work and ledge the rod on it, taking care that it is accurately lined up. Now take a pencil and scribe in the salient points on the whirling stock. For accurate location of the pencil I usually use a three-cornered file to make a series of V-grooves on the leading edge of the rod. Fig 13.9 shows the rod in use.

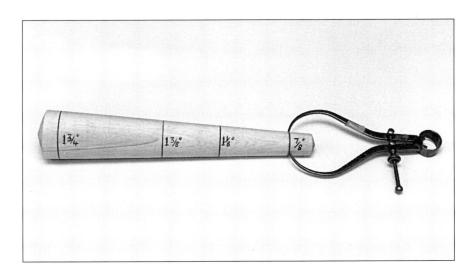

Fig 13.8 Typical sizing stick for use when only one set of calipers is available.

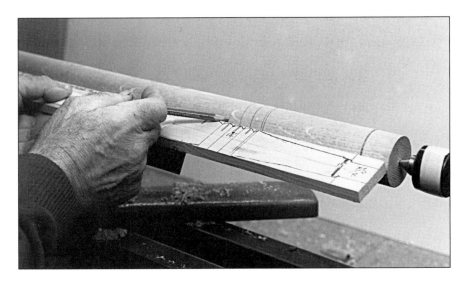

Fig 13.9 Making use of the marking stick to transfer the salient points on to the turned cylinder.

81

The other three sizing cuts can now be made. The parting tool is used in the one-handed mode and the caliper used in the other hand.

The most important sizing is the ⅞in (22mm) diameter spigot at the top of the legs that fit into the corresponding holes on the underside of the seat. These must be a good push fit. It should be noted that I have deliberately left a slight shoulder at the base of the spigot, which prevents the leg being hammered in too far and possibly breaking through the top of the seat.

Profiling can now commence, with the toe of the ½in (13mm) skew chisel being used to make V-cuts on the marks indicating the three beads near the top of the leg. The same tool can be used (either the toe or the heel) to develop them to the finished half-round profile. Alternatively, a parting tool or a spindle gouge can be used to achieve the same result. The taper between the beads and the ⅞in (22mm) spigot can then be formed with either a roughing-out gouge, spindle gouge or, if you are competent enough, a ½in (13mm) skew chisel.

The long taper between the bottom of the three beads and the 1⅜in (35mm) diameter *pointed* bead near the bottom of the leg is best formed with the roughing-out gouge. If this tool is very sharp, it will leave an acceptable

finish. You may prefer to finish the taper with a skew chisel but this tool does not necessarily guarantee a better finish, particularly on some timbers with pronounced interlocking grain.

In both cases, it will probably be necessary to steady the workpiece with one hand to prevent whip and the resultant spirally effect on the surface of the wood. Fig 13.10 shows a 1in (25mm) skew chisel being used.

The final shaping at the bottom of the leg is completed with the aid of the ½in (13mm) skew and the roughing-out gouge. I always think it advisable to make a slight chamfer at the very bottom of the leg to prevent break-out of the end grain.

The positions of the stretchers can now be marked on the leg. I prefer to use the toe of a skew chisel to make a slight V-cut, which not only assists accurate drill location but also adds to the visual appeal.

The leg can now be sanded, commencing with nothing coarser than 150 grit paper and going through various grades to about 320 grit. A handful of shavings applied to the whirling wood will burnish oak to a pleasing shine, and also highlight any scratches caused by careless sanding.

When satisfied with the finish, position the leg behind the lathe on a couple of V-blocks for reference and then make the other three legs to match.

Fig 13.10 Planing the long taper with a skew chisel, with the left hand being used as a steady.

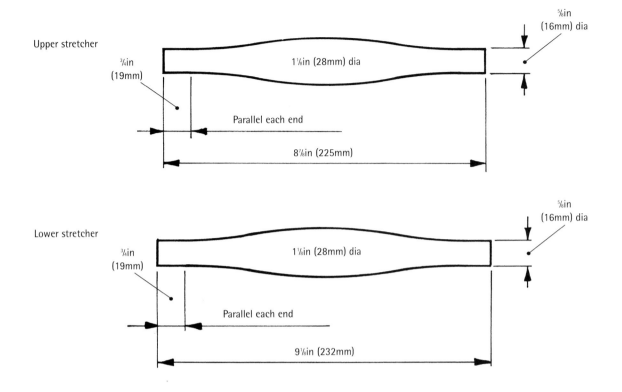

Upper stretcher

⁵⁄₈in (16mm) dia

¾in (19mm)

1⅛in (28mm) dia

Parallel each end

8⅞in (225mm)

Lower stretcher

⁵⁄₈in (16mm) dia

¾in (19mm)

1⅛in (28mm) dia

Parallel each end

9⅛in (232mm)

Fig 13.11 Dimensional details of the stretchers.

STRETCHERS

These are prepared from 1¼in (32mm) square stock. To take into account the splay of the legs, the upper stretcher is cut to a length of 8⅞in (225mm), and the lower one cut to 9⅛in (232mm) long. I use a ½in (13mm) diameter drive centre which allows me to cut the ⅝in (16mm) spigots without fouling the metal. The shape of the stretchers is simple, and the whole profile can be fashioned with a roughing-out gouge. It will be seen from Fig 13.11 that the last ¾in (19mm) at both ends is turned to a parallel ⅝in (16mm) diameter. This, of course, will be the spigot that fits into the corresponding-size hole to be bored in the legs. Repeat the sanding process on each.

BORING THE STRETCHER HOLES

Fig 13.12 shows a cut-away section of a leg and the relationship of the two blind stretcher holes. It will be necessary to fix the drilling jig at 90° to the fixing used when boring the holes in the underside of the seat. It would otherwise not be possible to bore the holes in the

required positions because the central pillar of the drilling machine would prevent it.

The two pegs in the V-block are located in the corresponding holes of the drilling jig, and the two 5°wedges inserted between the hinged tables. It is *vitally important* to arrange each leg to be bored so that the bottom of the leg is to the right when viewed from the front, otherwise the stretchers will leave the legs in the wrong plane! Fig 13.13 shows the correct set-up.

To provide accurate radial boring, the V-cradle must be positioned so that the centre point of the drill bit locates exactly in the centre of the V formed by the chamfers.

Start the process by boring the *lower* stretcher hole in all four legs to the required depth determined by the depth stop on the drill press.

The holes for the upper stretchers can now commence, but it is important to understand that we require (for the sake of a better expression) *two left-hand holes* and *two right-hand holes*.

Fig 13.12 Cut-away section of leg showing the 'blind' stretcher holes.

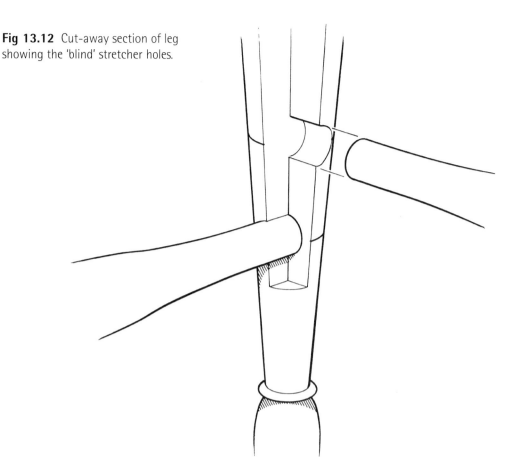

This can be achieved easily by inserting a short length of ⅝in (16mm) dowel in the previously bored lower stretcher hole and boring the upper hole in *two only* of the legs with the dowel *facing towards* the central pillar of the drill press and with the drill bit at 90° to the dowel (*see* Fig 13.14).

The two opposite-hand holes are drilled with the dowel *facing the operator* (*see* Fig 13.15). It all sounds very complicated but it isn't really, and careful study of Figs 13.13–13.15 should clarify the process.

ASSEMBLY

It is advisable to 'dry fit' all the component parts before glue is applied. I use a PVA glue, smearing each joint with a light application, commencing the assembly by fitting the legs into the seat holes (only about ¼in/6mm deep). By springing the legs open I am able to insert each stretcher in the leg holes so that they

'bottom'. The stool is then turned upside down (the top resting on a clean sheet of thick cardboard), and the legs carefully hammered home. If the jointing is good, there is no need to use clamping devices.

FINISHING

You may prefer to apply your choice of finish as each component part is completed on the lathe. A sealed and waxed finish lends itself to this choice, although great care must be taken to avoid wax getting on the joints before the gluing process. Another alternative is to use tung oil or Danish oil. It will probably require a minimum of three applications with a 24-hour interval between each coat, but the finish is extremely durable.

I choose to spray the completed project with two coats of sanding basecoat followed by the application of a soft paste wax, and am more than satisfied with the results.

Fig 13.13 Method of boring the *lower* stretcher hole. Note that, with the 5° wedges inserted from the end opposite the hinges, the bottom of the legs *must* be positioned to the right of the operator when viewed from the front.

Fig 13.14 Method of boring for the 'right-hand' *upper* stretcher. A ⅝in (16mm) dowel has been inserted in the previously bored lower hole. It must be positioned at 90° to the drill bit and *facing towards* the central pillar of the drill press.

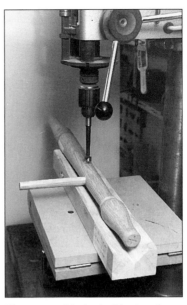

Fig 13.15 Method of boring for the 'left-hand' *upper* stretcher. This time the dowel must face in the opposite direction and towards the operator.

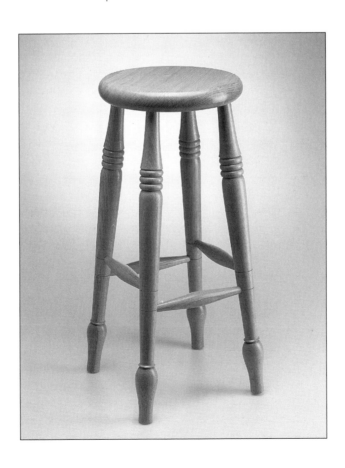

Chapter 14

Spinning Stool

TIME: 6 HOURS ★★★

This is one of the projects in the book in which not all the parts are made on the lathe. In fact, the only components made on the lathe are the four legs. Nevertheless, many woodturners are only too happy to make them, because they are a highly saleable commodity.

DESIGN CONSIDERATIONS

In years gone by, many stools were designed with three legs to overcome the problem of uneven floors. In this age of wall-to-wall carpeting, the need to combat instability has greatly reduced, so I make my stools with four legs because I consider them to be more pleasing to the eye.

The degree of difficulty involved in the making of the non-turned components should not be beyond the capabilities of the average woodworker. I nevertheless considered it best to include two different designs. Fig 14.1 shows a completed example of design 1.

Fig 14.1 The completed project (design 1).

Many woodturners do not possess a bandsaw and electric router, and the first design, Figs 14.2a and 14.2b, really requires both. The non-turned components on the second design, Figs 14.3a and 14.3b, can all be undertaken with hand tools, possibly making it a more appealing proposition.

The methods of turning, setting out, boring and jointing are identical in both designs.

CHOICE AND PREPARATION OF STOCK

I again chose oak for the example, but elm, beech, ash or mahogany are equally suitable. As with the bar stool, all the component parts should be cut from one board for best grain and colour effect. This is not always possible, however, so do not be reluctant to use offcuts from different boards.

ORDER OF WORK

SEAT

The drawings for the seat, back and wedge have been prepared on a grid system of 1in (25mm) squares, and simplify the making of full-size templates in card or thin sheet material. The overall seat dimensions (before shaping) are identical on both designs, i.e. 13½in x 11in (343mm x 279mm). The stock for the seat should be cut to size, squared up and accurately planed to a uniform thickness of approximately 1⅜in (35mm).

Commence by making a template for the seat in hardboard. This is cut to a rectangle measuring 13½in x 11in (343mm x 279mm). From the intended front edge of the seat, mark a distance of 11in (279mm) on one of the long sides and square this across the width to effectively form a square. Now draw diagonals, and from their intersection mark the position of each leg at $4\frac{1}{2}$in (114mm) from the centre mark (these diagonals will also serve as sight lines when boring the compound angles).

The outline profile of your choice can now be plotted, as can the position of the mortise to receive the back. Cut to shape by whatever means available, and finally drill a small hole on the hole centres for the legs, using a pointed awl when marking the underside of the seat. The template (design 1) should now look like that shown in Fig 14.4.

Place the template on the underside of the stock and mark the outline profile and the four hole centres. Now cut the outline profile on the bandsaw or with a handsaw. Note that the mortise is not marked on the underside.

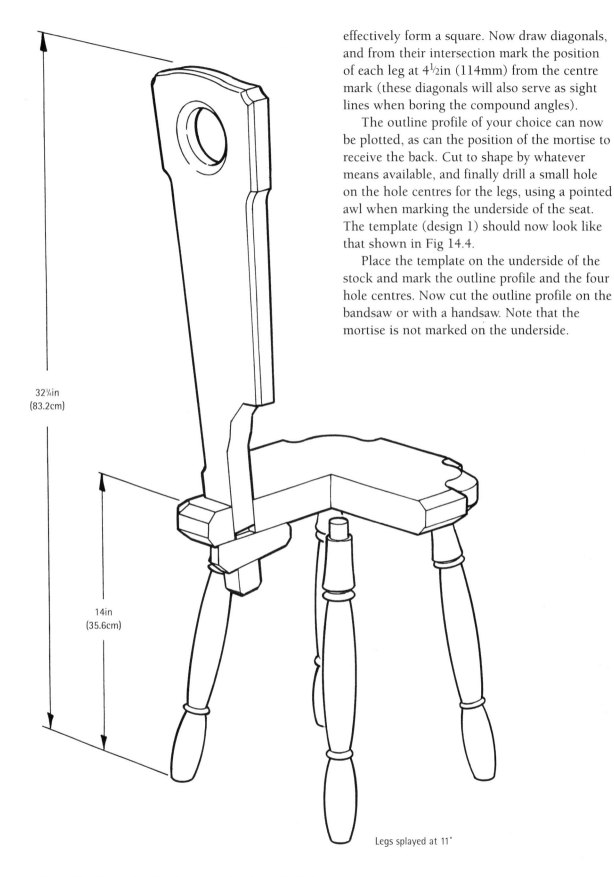

32¾in
(83.2cm)

14in
(35.6cm)

Legs splayed at 11°

Fig 14.2a Dimensional and constructional details, design 1.

Fig 14.2b Dimensional and constructional details, design 1.

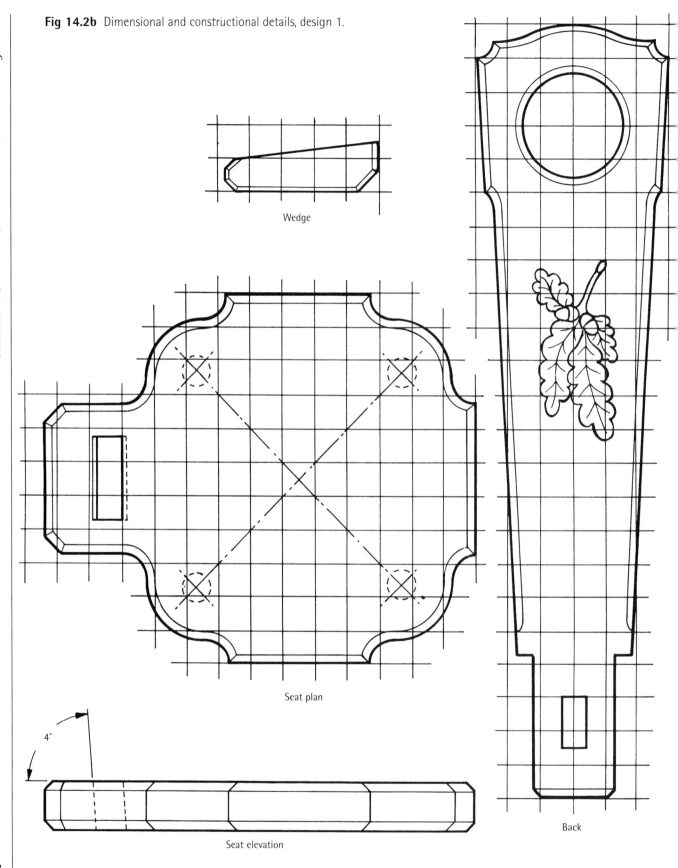

Wedge

Seat plan

4°

Seat elevation

Back

The next operation is to bore the four blind $\frac{7}{8}$in (22mm) holes to take the legs, so the depth stop on the drill must be adjusted to the required depth. Two 11° wedges are then prepared and inserted in the boring jig to give the required angle. The compound angle is achieved by lining up the diagonal marks with the central pillar of the drill press. Fig 14.5 should make this clear.

The mortise can now be marked on the *top* side of the seat with the aid of the template. The back is set at a rake of 4°, and accordingly two 4° wedges must be prepared for the boring jig. The drilling of these holes will remove the bulk of the waste from the $2\frac{1}{2}$in x $\frac{7}{8}$in (64mm x 22mm) mortise. Remember that they are through holes, so a piece of waste wood should be placed between the seat and the jig to prevent damage to the latter (*see* Fig 14.6).

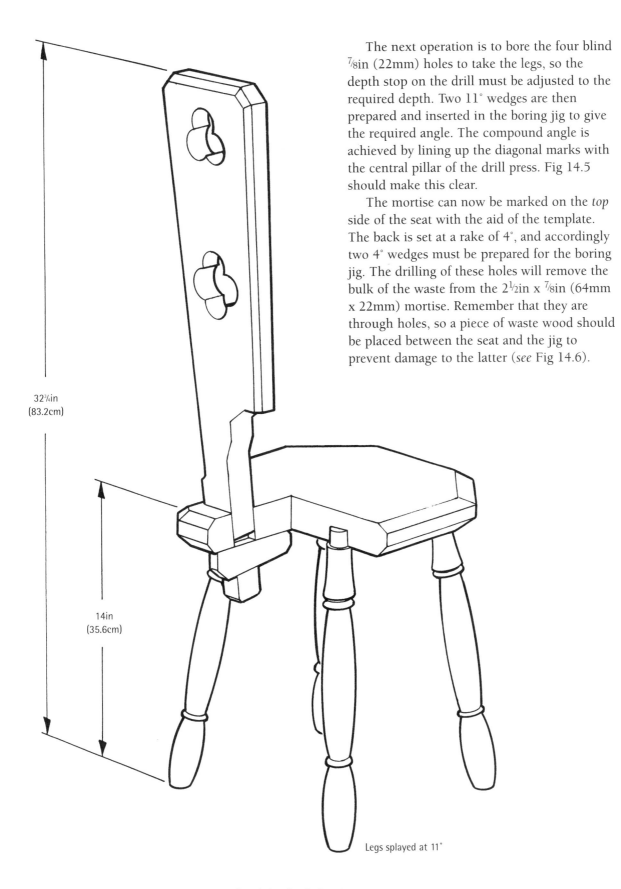

32¾in
(83.2cm)

14in
(35.6cm)

Legs splayed at 11°

Fig 14.3a Dimensional and constructional details, design 2.

Fig 14.3b Dimensional and constructional details, design 2.

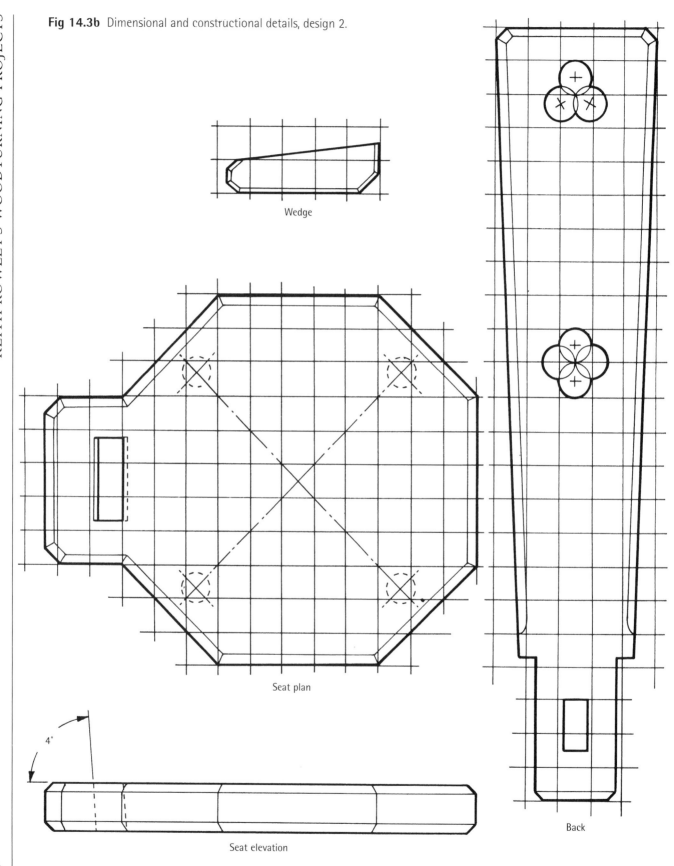

Wedge

Seat plan

Seat elevation

4°

Back

Fig 14.4 Typical seat template clearly showing the profile, hole centres and sight lines (design 1).

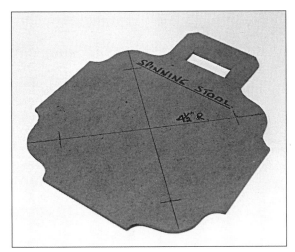

Fig 14.6 Boring the mortise from the seat top. Two 4° wedges are used. Note that a scrap piece of wood is inserted between seat and jig to prevent damage to the latter.

Fig 14.5 Boring the ⁷⁄₈in (22mm) holes in the underside of the seat. Note the 11° wedges inserted in the boring jig, and how the sight lines are lined up square to the central pillar of the drill press.

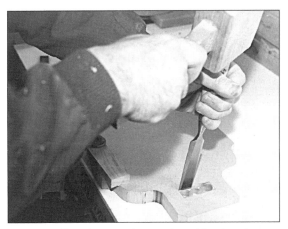

Fig 14.7 Squaring out the mortise with a bevel-edged chisel. The G-cramp and waste piece of wood securing the seat to the bench can just be seen beneath my right hand.

Continue by 'squaring out' the mortise with sharp chisels. Make sure that the chisel is inclined to the required 4° angle; light cuts should avoid any breakout of the fibres (*see* Fig 14.7).

The outer profile of the seat is now sanded to a smooth finish. This can be achieved by hand sanding or by making use of sanding drums fixed in the chuck of the drill press. My personal preference is for the quick-change sanding drums manufactured in four different diameters by Carrol Sanders Ltd (*see* page 162). They are not cheap, but they produce a super-smooth finish and save hours of hand sanding on both straight and curved profiles.

The chamfers on the edges of design 1 are worked with the electric router and appropriate-size cutter with guide pin. The chamfers on design 2 can be fashioned with a block plane, spokeshave and very sharp bevel-edge chisels. This completes the seat.

LEGS

These are produced from 1½in (38mm) square-section stock and can be cut to their finished length of 13½in (343mm). As with the bar stool legs, I suggest that a marking stick or rod be prepared to assist in the making of four matching profiles. A sizing stick (as shown in Fig 13.8 of the bar stool project) may also prove helpful. Careful study of Fig 14.8 should enable them to be produced with little trouble.

The turning of the legs can now follow the same procedures as those adopted for making the bar stool legs. After the stock has been reduced to the largest diameter, the rod is held up to the whirling wood and the salient points

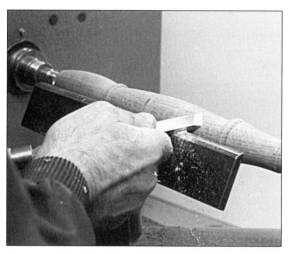

Fig 14.9 The ½in (13mm) skew chisel being used to plane the centre portion of a leg.

transferred with a pencil. Continue by sizing in the key diameters, and blend in the required profiles with gouges and chisels. Fig 14.9 shows a ½in (13mm) skew chisel (my favourite size) being used in the left-handed mode to refine the centre section of a leg.

It will be seen from Fig 14.8 that I have again opted for a slight shoulder at the bottom of the spigot that fits into the seat holes. This will prevent the possibility of the legs being hammered in too far and bursting through the top of the seat. Great care must be taken to ensure that each leg is a good tight fit, there being no stretchers to provide extra strength.

Repeat the sanding and burnishing process with shavings on each leg.

STOOL BACK

In addition to making an obvious back rest (canted backwards at an angle of 4°), it also makes the stool easier to handle and move about. On some designs the back is made a permanent fixture by gluing the tenon into the mortise and pegging it for extra strength.

I prefer the 'knock-down' design, and it will be seen from the drawings that the tenon protrudes through the bottom of the seat about 3in (76mm). This allows for a 1½in x ¾in (38mm x 19mm) mortise to be worked in it to take the wedge which secures it to the seat.

For design 1, prepare a piece of wood 24in (61cm) long x 6in (15.2cm) wide; for design 2, 24in (61cm) x 5in (12.7cm). Both require to be

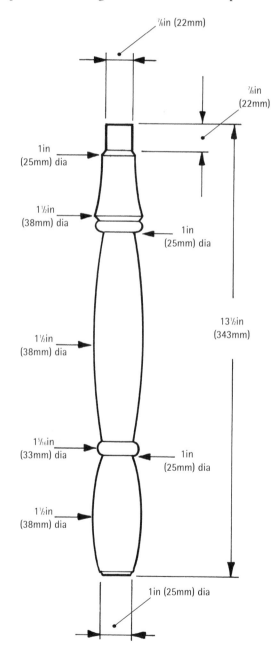

⅞in (22mm)

⅞in (22mm)

1in (25mm) dia

1½in (38mm) dia

1in (25mm) dia

13½in (343mm)

1½in (38mm) dia

1⁵⁄₁₆in (33mm) dia

1in (25mm) dia

1½in (38mm) dia

1in (25mm) dia

Fig 14.8 Dimensional details of the legs.

accurately thicknessed to a parallel ⅞in (22mm) to ensure a snug fit in the mortise.

Mark out the design of your choice from your previously constructed template, and either bandsaw or use hand tools to fashion the outline shape. *Remember* that the shoulders of the tenon need to be cut at an angle of 4° to suit the rake of the back. Fig 14.10 shows this being done with a tenon saw.

The mortise for the wedge is made by boring and squaring out with chisels (the same dimensions in both designs). The 3in (76mm) diameter hole near the top of design 1 can be bored or cut out with a jig saw or pad saw. If bored out (I used an expanding power bit in the pillar drill) it is *absolutely vital* that the stock is *securely clamped*.

The patterns in design 2 are overlapping 1in (25mm) diameter holes, three in the top pattern and four in the lower. These can be bored with a hand brace and bit if necessary (in any through-boring operation, it is important to clamp a piece of waste wood on the underside to prevent 'break-out').

The carving of the oak leaves and acorns on design 1 is optional (and it really could only be such a design on oak). I think it adds greatly to the appeal of the stool, and with practice it only takes a little over the hour to complete. The carving design is by courtesy of Christopher Milner Fine Woodcraft (*see* page 162).

The chamfers on the outer edges can now be worked either by using the electric router or by hand tools, as with the bar stool.

WEDGE

This is cut from a piece 5in x ¾in (127mm x 19mm) to the shape shown in the drawings. All the edges, with the exception of the top edge, look better if a slight chamfer is worked on them.

ASSEMBLY

First, dry fit the legs to the seat; when satisfied with the fit of each, apply a thin smear of glue in the holes and hammer the legs home. Continue by refining the fit of the tenon so that it is a snug fit in the seat mortise. The insertion of the wedge will pull the shoulders of the tenon on to the seat top, making the back good and secure.

FINISHING

Ensure that all components are well sanded down to about 320 grit before applying your choice of finish. It is advisable, whatever finish is used, to cut back the inevitably raised grain lightly with very fine abrasive between each coat.

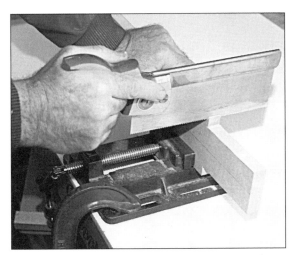

Fig 14.10 Making use of a small tenon saw to trim the tenon shoulders to the required 4° angle. Note the secure clamping method.

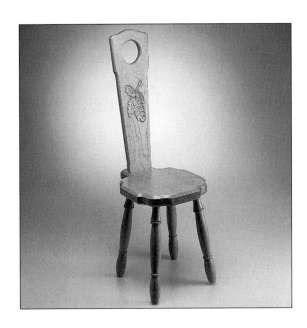

Chapter 15
Two-piece Hollow Forms

TIME: 1½ HOURS ★★★

Largely because of public demand, many demonstrations nowadays include advanced techniques on projects such as hollow forms, where large blocks of wood are used and the tools employed in the hollowing process look similar to instruments of medieval torture. It concerns me that having regard to the limited experience and skill of some of the onlookers, it is possible to underestimate the inherent dangers involved in this type of work, particularly if it is attempted with inadequate equipment.

I cannot emphasize too strongly, therefore, that some of the techniques employed on hollow-form projects can be dangerous unless a good deal of experience has been acquired in standard turning techniques.

The soundest advice I have heard in this respect came from professional woodturner Chris Stott. He recommends starting with miniature hollow forms (with which most hobby lathes and chucking systems will cope), using a set of three smallish yet sturdy tools which he has designed and markets (*see* pages 97 and 162).

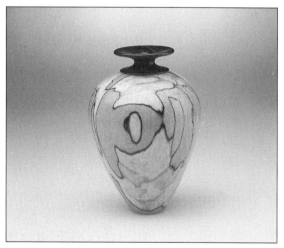

Fig 15.1 A completed piece in spalted beech and ebony.

You will be surprised at how quickly hollowing techniques can be acquired, and even more surprised at how relaxing and pleasurable the making of the forms can be.

DESIGN CONSIDERATIONS

Strictly speaking, hollow forms include end-grain turnings such as egg cups, goblets, vases and boxes. However, the modern woodworking definition seems to be the hollowing out of vessels through a small opening in the top. This means that most of the internal turning is done 'blind' and the turner must rely greatly on feel.

The smaller the aperture, the more difficult it is to obtain the required internal profile. Long necks should be avoided in the learning stage, as should 'squashed' shapes with acute shoulders. I quickly found that the bottle shape used in this example is the easiest to start with, and for me it has great visual appeal.

To make the hollowing even easier, I recommend the 'two-piece' form, which has the advantage of allowing the turner to work the internal shape through a larger hole than would generally be acceptable. This is cloaked by the 'planted' short end of contrasting-coloured wood, through which a small hole is bored. Fig 15.1 shows a completed example.

CHOICE AND PREPARATION OF STOCK

I think that the technique is more easily acquired when working end grain, and a good size to start with is that shown in Figs 15.2, 15.3 and 15.9. To make this, a block of wood measuring 4in (102mm) long by about 3in (76mm) square (grain running along the length) is required.

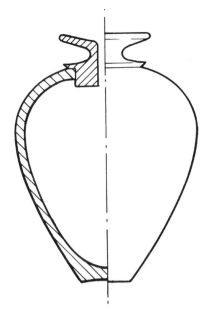

Fig 15.2 Part section showing the finished profile.

The choice of wood is important. In the learning stage, avoid using greasy, oily species such as olivewood, bocote and lignum vitae. These very quickly clog up the hole and the chippings are likely to wrap round the tool and cause it to spin violently. Instead, go for something not too dense. Spalted wood is particularly suitable, being light in weight and so giving the finished piece the 'feel-good factor', even when the walls are not as thin and even as you would have liked. Spalted beech is probably my favourite for this type of work, closely followed by spalted poplar, spalted

horse chestnut and brown oak. All look well with a contrasting-coloured piece of exotic wood 'planted' on the top.

ORDER OF WORK

Mount the stock between centres and, after reducing it to slightly over the finished diameter of 2¾in (70mm), form a spigot at one end to fit your choice of chuck. After chucking it will probably be necessary to make a few passes along the length of the piece with a roughing-out gouge to get it running dead true.

Continue by marking in the overall length of the body, that is, 3¼in (82mm) from the open end. Go in with a parting tool in the waste side to a diameter of about 1½in (38mm). *It is important* not to go any smaller with this sizing cut, or you will more than likely encounter vibration in the hollowing process to follow. Using a ⅜in (10mm) spindle gouge, the outside profile can now be fashioned, aiming for nice flowing curves.

For optimum visual appeal I think that, for a form of this size, the base diameter should finish at about ¾in (19mm). For this to be stable great attention must be given to making the walls very thin and even, otherwise the piece will be top-heavy, the slightest touch being enough to tip it over.

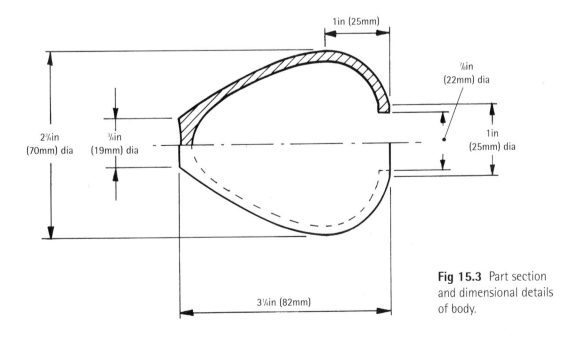

Fig 15.3 Part section and dimensional details of body.

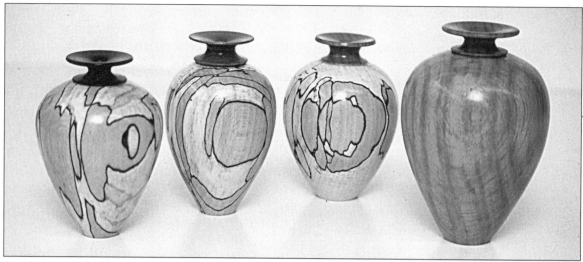

Fig 15.4 Four completed hollow forms – see text for design thoughts.

Fig 15.4 shows four hollow forms. The one on the extreme left, in spalted beech, has a ¾in (19mm) diameter base. The next two, also in spalted beech, have a 1in (25mm) base. I feel they look all right, but the one with the smaller base allows a nicer curve to be developed. The one on the extreme right in brown oak also has a 1in (25mm) base, but because the body of the form is larger (4in x 3¼in/102mm x 82mm), I think it looks better proportioned.

Considerable time can be saved on the hollowing process if part of the waste is bored out. In this example I made use of a ¾in (19mm) sawtooth cutter and Jacobs chuck fixed in the tailstock. A piece of tape stuck on the cutter shank at the appropriate place

ensured that I did not bore the hole too deep. At this stage the project should look something like that shown in Fig 15.5.

Still more waste can be removed without resorting to the special tools. A ⅜in (10mm) spindle gouge with a long bevel can be employed successfully near the top to about halfway down the inside. A similar tool with a very short bevel will also quickly remove a good deal of waste from the remainder.

Now to the three special tools shown in Fig 15.6. They are scrapers, and therefore they should be used in the 'trailing' mode. The tip on the straight cutter is aligned with the axis of the tool. The side-cutting tool has the tip fixed almost at right angles to the axis of the tool,

Fig 15.5 The partly completed main body. The outside has been profiled and a ¾in (19mm) hole has been bored down the centre to the required depth before using the special tools (note the tape on the cutter to ensure the correct hole depth).

Fig 15.6 The set of three hollowing tools by Chris Stott. From left to right: the crook-shanked tool, the straight tool and the side-cutting tool.

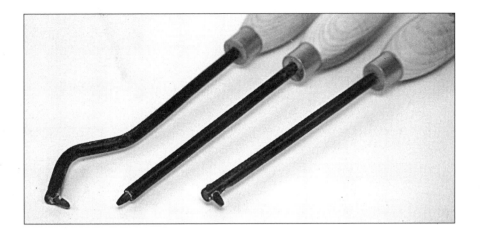

and the last tool is similar but the tool bar is crook-shanked so that the cutting tip can reach acutely shaped and undercut profiles, especially near the top of the forms.

Make sure they are kept sharp. I have found that a slip stone (a small, triangular-shaped oilstone) is as good as anything to keep them in good order.

Starting with the straight tool, remove as much waste as you can using minimum pressure to obtain a cut. The side-pointing tool, which is probably the most used of the three, can then be used to develop as even a wall as possible. After a little practice you will acquire a feel for the job and also be able to visualize exactly where the tip is cutting, despite not being able to see it. By using a nice swinging action, the outside profile can be followed very successfully.

The area adjacent to the hole will probably require the use of the crook-shanked tool. It is important to remember that the straight portion of the shank *must* be positioned on the tool rest as shown in Fig 15.7. Using it as shown in Fig 15.8, with the cranked section on the tool rest, will inevitably result in the tool being twisted violently in your hands.

It will be necessary to stop the lathe frequently to remove the waste and also to check the wall thickness. I use a bent piece of coat-hanger wire to remove the chippings, and a set of double-ended calipers to check the wall thickness. You may find these procedures tiresome and irritating, but it must be done to avoid disaster.

Until a little experience is acquired, I would suggest that the wall thickness should not be less than $\frac{1}{4}$in (6mm). It may also be advisable

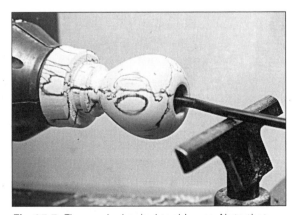

Fig 15.7 The crook-shanked tool in use. Note that the tool rest is positioned sufficiently far away from the wood so as to allow the straight part of the bar to be supported on it.

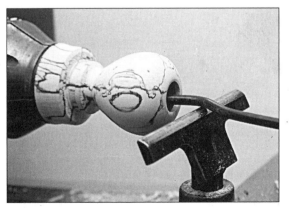

Fig 15.8 *Incorrect use* of the crook-shanked tool. The rest is too close to the wood, with the crook bearing on the tool rest. In this position the tool will be uncontrollable and may twist violently.

Fig 15.9 Part-sectioned detail and dimensions of the 'plant'.

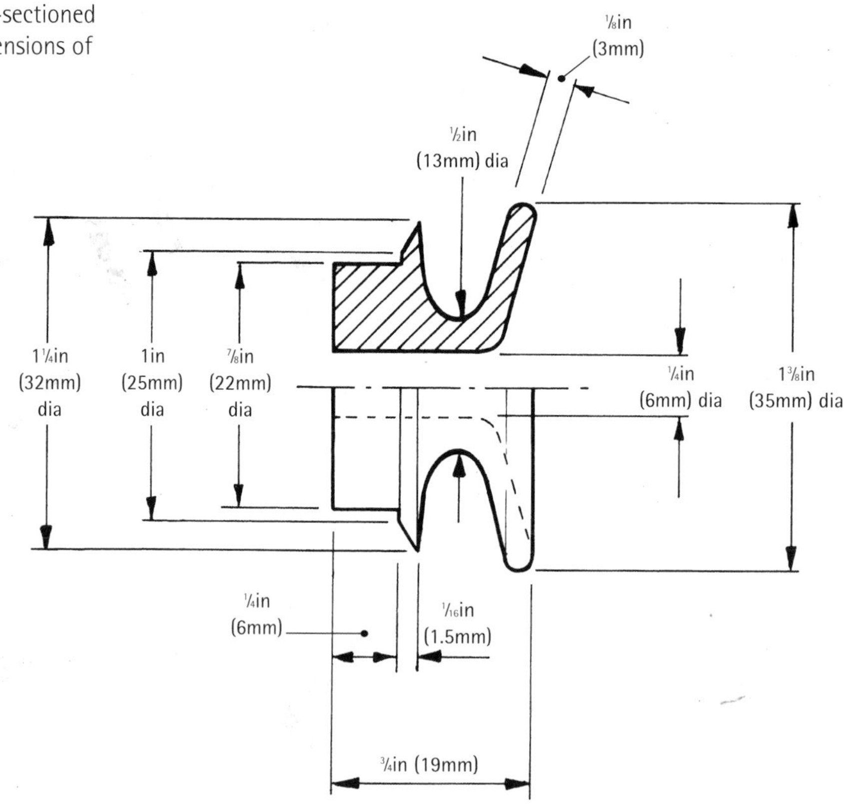

to leave the area near the base slightly thicker to assist stability. Having satisfactorily achieved a constant wall thickness, it will no doubt be necessary to clean up the edge of the hole as it is more than likely that it will have been damaged in the hollowing process. This can be done with a sharp skew chisel held flat on the rest and used scraper fashion. It is vital that this cut is dead parallel to the axis to ensure a good fit for the $\frac{7}{8}$in (22mm) spigot to be turned on the 'planted' piece.

Before removing the body from the lathe it is necessary to create a narrow flat area (about $\frac{1}{16}$in/1.5mm wide) immediately adjacent to the hole to match the square shoulder to be formed on the underside of the 'planted' piece. To ensure true running when the body is replaced in the chuck, I pencil in two marks near the bottom which line up with two corresponding pop marks on the chuck. This is described fully in Chapter 5 (*see* page 21).

You can now turn your attention to making the 'planted' piece (*see* Fig 15.9). For the example I made use of an off-cut of 2in (51mm) square ebony which I initially

mounted between centres. After reducing it to a cylinder, a spigot was cut at one end enabling it to be driven in the same chuck as I used for the main body.

With the aid of a set of verniers, measure the diameter of the hole in the top of the main body (about $\frac{7}{8}$in/22mm) and cut the corresponding spigot on the 'planted' piece. This must not be overtight or you run the risk of splitting the top. Now form another spigot immediately adjacent to the first one but about $\frac{1}{4}$in (6mm) larger in diameter. A slight chamfer is then formed with a small gouge on this second spigot, to leave a square shoulder of $\frac{1}{16}$in (1.5mm) deep which abuts the flat section worked on the side of the hole on the main body. By using the Jacobs chuck in the tailstock, a $\frac{1}{4}$in (6mm) hole can now be bored through its full length. Fig 15.10 shows how the 'planted' piece should look at this stage.

Remount the main body in the chuck, apply a dab of glue to the joint, and now make use of the tailstock with a live centre fitted to clamp the two together, making sure the grain is aligned to your satisfaction.

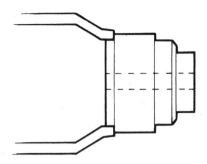

Fig 15.10 How the 'planted' piece should look after the initial sizing. This method allows for the body to be offered up to test the fit of the spigot. Note that the central ¼in (6mm) hole should be bored before removing from the chuck.

If the joint is good you need only wait a few minutes before completing the profile on the 'plant'. First, the excess length can be parted off (the tailstock still supporting it), followed by the profiling. For this, I used a ¼in (6mm) spindle gouge with swept-back wings which allowed me to form the deep, narrow cove and the slightly indented profile from the rim to the ¼in (6mm) hole with ease. Fig 15.11 shows the gouge in use making a refining cut in this area.

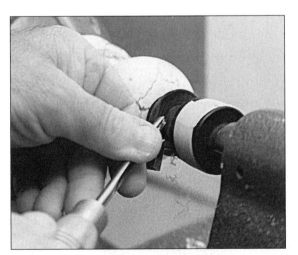

Fig 15.11 Refining the shape of the 'plant' with a ¼in (6mm) spindle gouge. Note that the tailstock is being used to support the piece.

FINISHING

The sanding process can now commence, and it is advisable to slow the lathe speed down to avoid too much heat being generated and running the risk of creating 'heat cracks' in the thin wall. For the same reason, do not start with too fine an abrasive. I used 120, 180, 240 and 320 grits.

Your choice of finish can now be applied. I chose to finish with two coats of sanding sealer, cut back with 600 grit wet or dry paper, followed by a very light application of friction polish and wax.

PARTING OFF

It is very easy when parting through spalted wood to 'pluck' a hole through the bottom of the main body. This can be avoided if a very narrow parting tool is used to minimize the resistance by the wood fibres. A narrow hacksaw blade suitably ground is ideal for this purpose.

Alternatively, and perhaps the best way, is to stop the parting cut short and complete the severance with a fine-toothed saw. In both cases, a little manicuring is required with a small sanding pad, and ideally the base should be slightly concaved for stability.

With some experience in making these small hollow forms, there is no reason why you should not be a little more adventurous and go on to make larger and more difficult shapes. It will be necessary, of course, to acquire the longer and stronger hollowing tools and a lathe sufficiently robust to cope with them safely.

Chapter 16
Gavel and Anvil

TIME: 3¼ HOURS ★ ★ ★

The potential for the sale of gavels is enormous – from High Court judges, chairmen of large companies, organizations like the Freemasons and Rotary Clubs, and right through to the other end of the spectrum such as chairpersons of working men's clubs, sports clubs and a multitude of similar organizations. All make use of a gavel and anvil either as a ceremonial piece or for calling to order.

If, therefore, the order book is not looking too healthy, a visit to the local information centre, from which details of club officials are usually available, could well prove rewarding.

DESIGN CONSIDERATIONS

Having regard to this potential, I find it strange that I do not ever recall seeing in a book or magazine a design and instructions for the making of this most useful project.

The gavel is a replica of one used by a judge on a former Assize Circuit, but the anvil or block is my own design and it is larger than many you see. In addition to making it more stable, it is sufficiently large to create a recess in which the gavel head sits and balances when not in use. The rim of the recess also elevates the handle well clear of the table, enabling the user to pick it up quickly and easily.

CHOICE AND PREPARATION OF STOCK

It is essential to choose a hard, heavy and close-grained wood. I chose ebony for the gavel, and because I did not have a piece in this species large enough to make the anvil, I decided to use maple, a hard, contrasting-coloured wood, into which I inlaid an ebony striking plate. It will be seen that I have 'planted' a maple tip on

the end of the handle, and I also drove a maple wedge in the joint to enhance the contrasting theme. The wedge, of course, when combined with the gluing process, makes for an exceptionally strong joint, which is absolutely vital or the head will soon work loose.

The head is prepared from a piece of ebony measuring 4in (102mm) long x 2½in (64mm) square. For the handle a piece measuring 7½in (191mm) long x 1½in (38mm) square is required. The maple used for the base, from 7in (178mm) x 1¾in (44mm) stock, should have one side planed flat and true and then bandsawn to size. The ebony striking plate is an off-cut of 2in (51mm) square material.

ORDER OF WORK

The photographs and drawings should be carefully studied before making a start. Fig 16.1 shows the completed project; you can see how the gavel head rests in the recess cut in the base.

Fig 16.1 The completed project.

Fig 16.2 The gavel has been removed from the anvil to provide a clearer view of the ebony striking plate and wedge.

Fig 16.2 shows the anvil with the gavel removed, providing a clearer view of the ebony striking plate and the maple wedge.

Fig 16.3 shows the assembled gavel, the method of jointing the maple 'plant' at the bottom of the handle and the wedge securing the head.

HEAD

Commence by making the head (*see* Fig 16.4). Accurate setting-out for centring and boring the through hole to receive the handle is absolutely vital. Use a carpenter's marking gauge to scribe dead centre on both ends and one face. Then bore the ½in (13mm) hole in the still square section on the pillar drill (a power drill or a hand brace will suffice if care is taken).

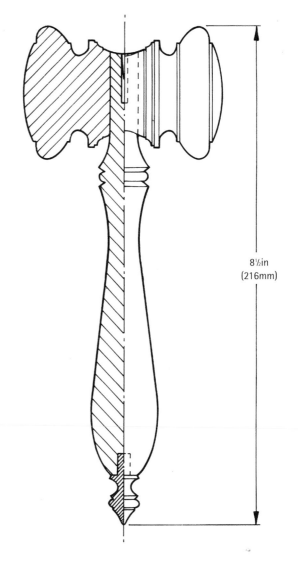

8½in (216mm)

Fig 16.3 Constructional details of the gavel, 'plant' and wedge.

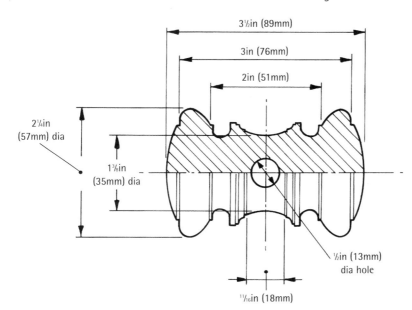

3½in (89mm)

3in (76mm)

2in (51mm)

2¼in (57mm) dia

1⅜in (35mm) dia

½in (13mm) dia hole

1¹⁄₁₆in (18mm)

Fig 16.4 Dimensional details of the gavel head.

101

Fig 16.5 shows an example of a head that has been prepared in this way and the boring operation in progress. (A piece of scrap whitewood has been used for the photograph so that the marking out can be better seen – marks do not show up too well on ebony. For the same reason, walnut has been used for the gavel head in the sequence photographs.)

Fig 16.5 Typical gavel head showing the central hole being bored. Note the gauge marks (pencilled in for clarity) on the end and face, which provide for accurate location of centres and the boring operation.

Continue by mounting the blank between centres and, after reducing it to a cylinder with a roughing-out gouge, form a 1½in (38mm) diameter spigot at the tailstock end to fit the corresponding jaws of your chuck. After transferring to the chuck, true the piece up to slightly over the intended maximum diameter of 2¼in (57mm).

The main features of the design are then marked on the whirling wood with the aid of a marking stick (prepared from the drawing). To achieve exactness of copying either side of the central hole, I think it best to use a 'half stick' to set out. The centre mark on the stick is lined up with the centre of the hole and the salient

points pencilled on to the workpiece. The marking stick is then turned end-for-end and the other side of the hole is marked. Fig 16.6 shows the marking stick in use.

The fillets on both sides of the large beads on the ends are 1½in (38mm) in diameter. These four sizing cuts can be made first, followed by the 1¾in (44mm) sizing cuts immediately adjacent to the coves. The blank should then look something like that shown in Fig 16.7.

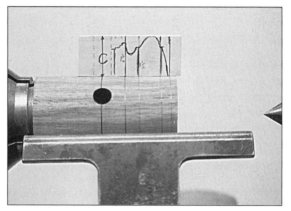

Fig 16.6 Setting out the design profiles with the aid of a 'half' marking stick.

Fig 16.7 What the blank should look like after the initial sizing cuts have been made.

It is important to complete as much of the shaping as possible on this first fixing, because when the piece is reverse chucked it will only be gripping on the very narrow fillet of ⅟₁₆in (1.5mm) at the extreme end. Take care to make the profiles as balanced as possible either side of the centre hole or the whole effect will be ruined. I used a ¼in (6mm) spindle gouge for the bulk of the profiling, finishing with a ⅛in (3mm) parting tool to cut the fillets nice and crisp.

Fig 16.8 shows the gouge being used to refine the radius on the end of the head. Note that almost all the profiling has been completed on the initial chucking.

Fig 16.8 The rounding over of the 'open' end being refined with a ¼in (3mm) spindle gouge. Note that almost all the profiling has been done on this initial chucking.

After sanding down to about 320 grit, your choice of finish can be applied. When dry the piece is reverse chucked, and it is not a bad idea to pack the chuck with some thin cloth or paper towel to avoid damaging the polish. The final profiling on the head can now be done by

Fig 16.9 A completed gavel head clearly showing the centre hole.

forming the radius on the other end of the head and then repeating the sanding and polishing process.

Fig 16.9 shows a completed gavel head, the through hole clearly visible.

HANDLE

Dimensional details are provided in Fig 16.10. The first operation is to bore a ¼in (6mm) diameter hole by about ⅜in (10mm) deep in one end to take the maple 'plant'. The method of using the Jacobs chuck in the headstock to do this has been described previously (*see* page 32).

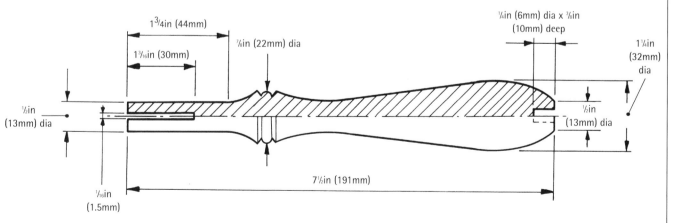

Fig 16.10 Dimensional and jointing details of the handle.

I again made use of the Chapman light-pull drive in the headstock, with the hole in the blank running on a live centre. The stock can be reduced to a cylinder and the shoulder at the tailstock end squared off with the toe of a skew chisel to give a good joint with the 'plant'.

The short end for the 'plant' (*see* Fig 16.11) was driven between centres and a ¼in (6mm) diameter spigot formed with a parting tool. Glue in position, and the assembled blank should now look similar to the example shown in Fig 16.12.

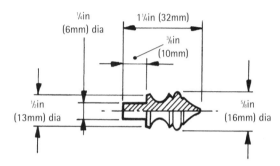

Fig 16.11 Dimensional details of the maple 'plant'.

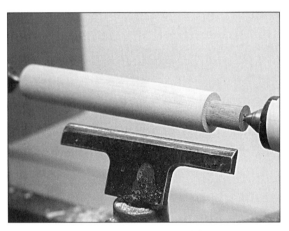

Fig 16.12 A typical handle prepared for turning between centres. The main body has been bored at one end with a ¼in (6mm) diameter hole, and the contrasting-coloured 'plant' has been glued in position.

The whole profiling can now follow, with particular attention being given to the accurate sizing of the top 2in (51mm) to a ½in (13mm) diameter so as to ensure a good push fit into the head. Sand and polish (avoiding the portion forming the joint) and carefully part off at the 'plant' end.

The saw cut to take the wedge can be done with a fine handsaw or on the bandsaw. Be careful not to go too deep or the saw kerf will be visible underneath the head. The wedge (*see* Fig 16.13) can be cut by hand or on a bandsaw from a piece of ½in (13mm) thick stock.

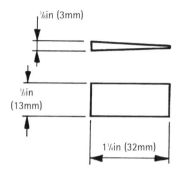

Fig 16.13 Dimensional details of the wedge.

ASSEMBLY

Apply a thin smear of glue on the inside of the hole and press the handle into position. The wedge should be positioned *across the grain* of the head, or you run the risk of splitting it. Fig 16.14 shows the wedge being hammered in. When the glue has dried, the bulk of the waste wood protruding through the top of the joint can be removed with a coping saw and then blended in to the hollow profile with a fine round file and abrasives.

Fig 16.14 The wedge being hammered into the saw kerf cut into the handle. Note it has been positioned *across* the grain of the head to prevent splitting.

BASE

After bandsawing to size, a 1³⁄₈in (35mm) diameter hole is drilled to a depth of ⅛in (3mm) in the centre of the underside to fit on the expanding jaws of your chosen chuck. The edges are then trued up and the face dressed off with a ³⁄₈in (10mm) bowl gouge. The next stage is to form the 3¼in x ³⁄₈in (82mm x 10mm) deep recess, and this is done with a parting tool and flattened with a square-ended scraper. The 1³⁄₈in (35mm) diameter x ¼in (6mm) deep recess to take the striking plate is similarly worked, followed by the profiling of the edge with a ³⁄₈in (10mm) spindle gouge and parting tool for the fillets.

Fig 16.15 (plan view of the upper side) and Fig 16.16 (section through the base) provide all the relevant profiling details.

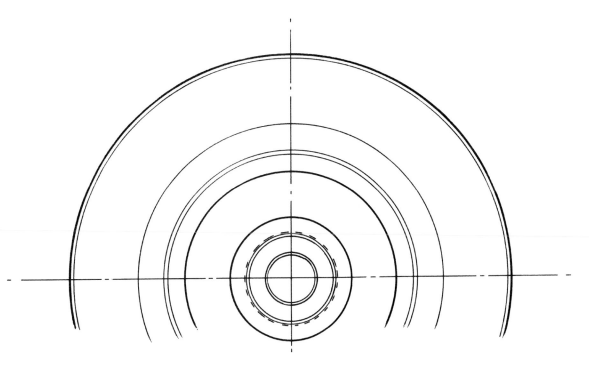

Fig 16.15 Plan view of the upper side of the base.

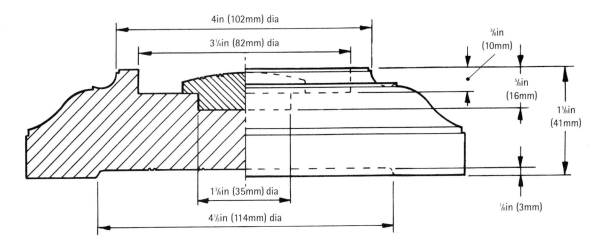

Fig 16.16 Section through base and dimensional details.

Fig 16.17 shows the upper side of the base completed to this particular stage and before the sanding and polishing process.

The recess to take the striking plate can be used to reverse chuck the piece on to a softwood jam chuck, enabling the 4½in (114mm) recess to be formed on the underside (thus removing the initial means of chucking) and also facilitating the use of the toe of a skew

chisel to cut the four shallow concentric lines shown in Figs 16.16 and 16.18 (plan view of underside).

STRIKING PLATE

Fig 16.19 provides dimensional details. Commence by mounting a short end of 2in (51mm) square stock between centres, and form a spigot at one end to fit the chuck. After transferring to the chuck, cut the spigot to fit in the central recess (1⅜in/35mm diameter x ¼in/6mm deep). Again, this needs to be a good push fit. The piece then needs to be reverse chucked again to allow the top of the striking plate to be rounded over and the decorative lines cut in with the toe of the skew chisel. Fig 16.20 shows this final operation.

FINISHING

You may wish to apply your choice of finish as each component part is made, and this is fine as long as the parts forming the joints are not coated. An alternative would be to seal and oil after the project has been completed. I chose to spray finish mine with a tough melamine-based lacquer.

Fig 16.17 Upperside of the base completed and ready for reverse chucking.

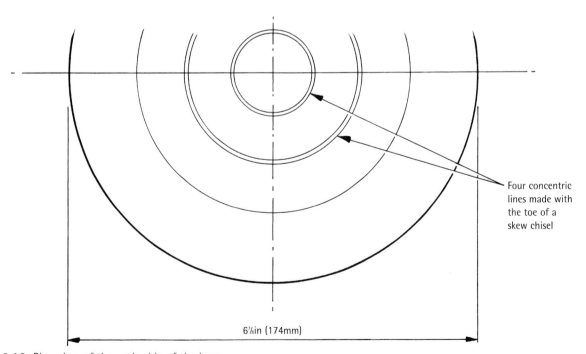

Four concentric lines made with the toe of a skew chisel

6⅞in (174mm)

Fig 16.18 Plan view of the underside of the base.

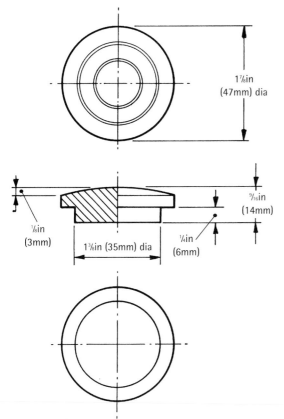

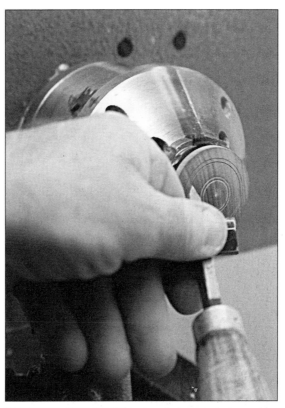

1⁷⁄₈in (47mm) dia

⁹⁄₁₆in (14mm)

¹⁄₈in (3mm)

1³⁄₈in (35mm) dia

¹⁄₄in (6mm)

Fig 16.19 Striking plate details.

Fig 16.20 The toe of the skew being used to cut the concentric lines on the top face of the striking plate.

Chapter 17
Birthday Boxes

TIME: 2½ HOURS ★★★★

Although astrology has now lost much of its former credibility, the daily ritual of reading one's horoscope in the papers is practised by thousands.

The exploitation of such superstitions is evident by the great number of artefacts on which the signs of the zodiac appear. Why not, therefore, try to boost your order book by making 'birthday boxes' with some kind of inlaid zodiac sign? You may well be pleasantly surprised at the response.

DESIGN CONSIDERATIONS

The inlaid sign is probably best done on the top of a box, and more easily achieved if the box lid is flat. A flat base goes very well with a flat top, as do parallel sides: in other words, a cylinder with a lid size in proportion to the main body should produce an attractive, highly saleable box.

A marquetry inlay can be used by those having the skill to prepare one. I chose the simpler method of inlaying a thin sycamore disc on which the birthday sign had been burned (pyrography). Fig 17.1 shows a completed box, and Fig 17.2 shows the box with the lid removed.

Fig 17.3 shows a part section of the whole box, and Figs 17.4 and 17.5 provide dimensional details. All need to be studied carefully before commencing the project.

CHOICE AND PREPARATION OF STOCK

With sycamore being used for the inlay, it is necessary to choose a contrasting-coloured hardwood for the box. In addition to choosing a species that is visually appealing, it is important that the wood is bone dry and noted for stability. I therefore decided on a piece of nice, dry padauk which satisfies these requirements.

To make the box in the example, a piece of 3in (76mm) square section x 3½in (89mm) long is needed. The zodiac sign was done by pyrographer Bob Neil (*see* page 162).

Fig 17.1 The completed box.

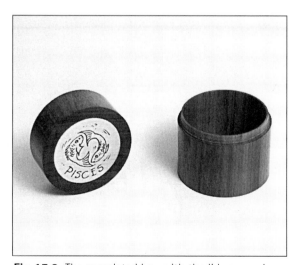

Fig 17.2 The completed box with the lid removed.

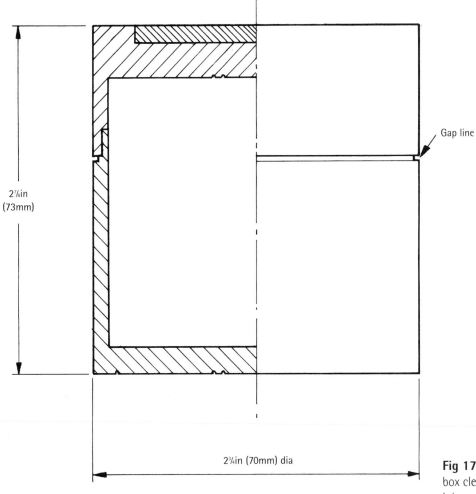

2⁷⁄₈in
(73mm)

Gap line

2³⁄₄in (70mm) dia

Fig 17.3 Part section of box clearly showing the inlay and gap line.

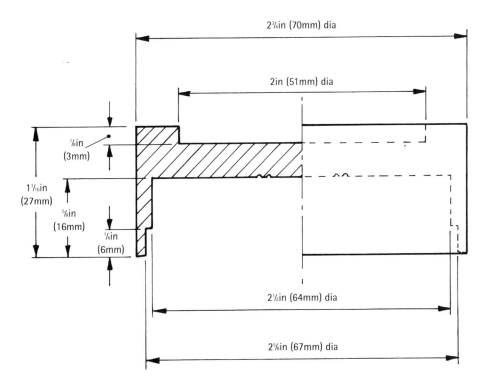

2³⁄₄in (70mm) dia

2in (51mm) dia

¹⁄₈in
(3mm)

1¹⁄₁₆in
(27mm)

⁵⁄₈in
(16mm)

¹⁄₄in
(6mm)

2¹⁄₂in (64mm) dia

2⁵⁄₈in (67mm) dia

Fig 17.4 Part section and dimensional details of lid.

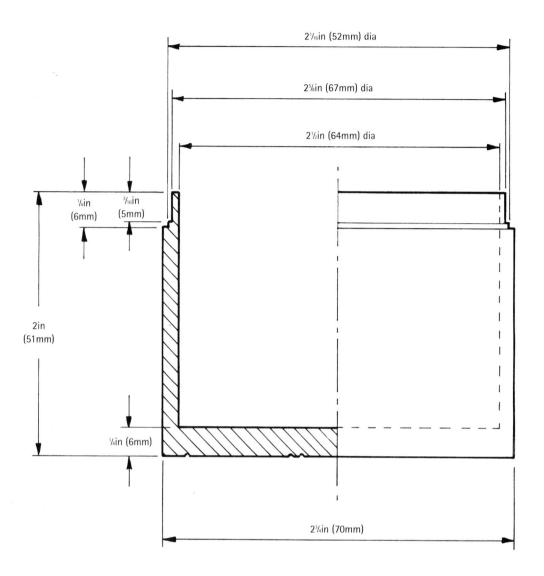

2¹⁄₁₆in (52mm) dia

2⅝in (67mm) dia

2½in (64mm) dia

¼in (6mm)

³⁄₁₆in (5mm)

2in (51mm)

¼in (6mm)

2¾in (70mm)

Fig 17.5 Part section and dimensional details of main body.

ORDER OF WORK

SYCAMORE INLAY

By referring to Fig 17.4 it will be seen that the sycamore inlay is finished to a diameter of 2in (51mm). Unfortunately, the stock size of the sycamore discs is 4in (102mm) diameter, and accordingly they must be accurately reduced so as to ensure that the burnt design remains central.

After careful setting-out, cut the disc to slightly over the required diameter on the bandsaw and, using double-sided tape, secure it centrally to a dead size 2in (51mm) spigot

turned on a piece of scrap softwood. It is then a simple matter to reduce it to the same diameter with a spindle gouge. In order to ensure a good fit in the recess to be formed in the top of the lid, be careful to cut the edge with just a hint of a taper from front to underside. Fig 17.6 shows such an inlay secured to the scrapwood spigot and turned to size. Also shown is another sycamore disc of the original diameter.

Before removing from the chuck, apply two coats of sanding sealer, and cut back with 600 grit paper. This process prevents the red dust from the padauk contaminating the disc in the subsequent sanding operation.

The box lid (the shortest length) is then transferred to the spigot chuck, trued up with light cuts with a sharp gouge and followed by the forming of the rebate (to form the joint with the main body). The bulk of the waste wood is removed with a ³⁄₈in (10mm) spindle gouge, ground with a short bevel, and squared out with a ¹⁄₂in (13mm) side and end cutting scraper, the profile of which is shown in Fig 17.8. This tool allows you to cut a crisp right angle where the wall and bottom merge. The top of the lid is left thicker than normal (*see* Fig 17.4) to accommodate the sycamore inlay.

Fig 17.6 The inlay has been secured to a scrapwood spigot with double-sided tape and turned to the required diameter. Also shown is another inlay of the original diameter.

Fig 17.7 The stock has been mounted between centres, reduced to a cylinder, and a spigot formed at each end to fit the choice of chuck. Note also the pencil line indicating the lid cut-off point.

BOX

The stock is first mounted between centres. After reducing it to a cylinder with a roughing-out gouge, form a 2in (51mm) spigot at both ends to fit the largest jaws of your chuck. The size of the lid is also pencilled in. Fig 17.7 shows a box completed to this stage.

In order to minimize grain mis-match, adopt the normal procedure for box making and cut the cylinder into two pieces on the bandsaw (fine blade). Of course, a parting tool can be used for the same purpose but obviously grain alignment can be a problem.

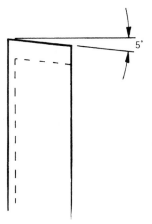

Fig 17.8 Profile of side and end cutting scraper.

Fig 17.9 shows the side and end cutting scraper in use, and Fig 17.10 shows the inside of the lid being tested for flatness with a scrap of wood (with the lathe stationary). Careful sanding can then follow (the rebate forming the joint should not be sanded or sealed, otherwise a well-fitting lid is unlikely), and a couple of coats of sealer should be applied, cut back and then waxed.

With the main body of the box now fixed in the chuck, continue by forming the spigot to fit the lid on a good push fit. My method is to use the parting tool in the one-handed mode and hold the lid in the other, offering it up until it just leads on to the spigot. Fig 17.11 clearly shows this method of working.

Both hands can now be used to make the spigot the required width and refine the diameter for the desired fit. This must be tight enough to drive the lid when recessing for the inlay, but not so tight as to be difficult to remove.

The top of the lid can now be faced off to the finished size. My choice of tool for this is always a ⅜in (10mm) spindle gouge, and with practice a clean, flat surface is possible. The recess for the inlay can then be set out with dividers and removed with a gouge and the side and end cutting scraper.

Stop the lathe and test the fit frequently, as the whole effect will be spoilt with a bad joint. The depth of the recess should allow the inlay to sit slightly below the level of the surrounding padauk so that, in the subsequent sanding process, only the padauk requires sanding and not the previously sealed sycamore.

Fig 17.12 shows an inlay about to be test-fitted into the recess before being secured with a dab of PVA glue.

For reasons mentioned later, I think it best not to sand the lid at this stage, so it can now be removed allowing a 'gap line' to be cut about ¹⁄₁₆in (1.5mm) wide and the same depth immediately adjacent to the spigot on the main body of the box. The purpose of this is to prevent the seeing or feeling of any distortion that may follow in the event of any subsequent shrinkage.

Fig 17.9 The inside of the lid has been hollowed out and the side and end cutting scraper is being used to square off the walls and base.

Fig 17.10 Testing the inside of the box lid for flatness. **Caution:** the lathe must be switched off for this operation.

Fig 17.11 The lid being offered up to the main body as the parting tool is used one-handed to form the spigot to fit the corresponding rebate on the lid.

Fig 17.12 The lid has been fitted to the body with a 'drive' fit, and the recess has been formed to take the sycamore inlay on a push fit.

Continue by removing the bulk of the waste wood from the inside with a gouge, followed by the use of the side and end cutting scraper to form the parallel walls and flat bottom. Now sand, seal and wax the completed inside, followed by measuring the depth and transferring it to the outside. Make a shallow parting cut in the wastewood side of this mark and to the required base thickness.

The lid can now be refitted and the whole cylinder trued up with light cuts with a newly sharpened roughing-out gouge. The outside and the top of the lid can now be sanded, sealed and waxed. The reason for leaving the sanding of the lid until this stage is to preserve the snug-fitting lid – sanding the outside of the lid at the earlier stage before the removal of the waste from the inside of the main body can result in uneven shrinkage, causing a loose fit.

The fit of the lid can now be refined. I do not like over-tight lids (and in my experience, neither does the buying public, particularly senior citizens and people with arthritic hands). This, however, is no excuse for a lid that drops off when the box is held upside down.

The final operation is to reverse the main body of the box to clean up the underneath.

For this, prepare a softwood jam-fit chuck, carefully cutting a recess to receive the inverted box on a *gentle* push fit. Making this too tight could split the box.

Fig 17.13 shows the box jammed on to the chuck and a spindle gouge being used to clean off the base, which is best cut slightly concave in the interests of stability.

Fig 17.13 The main body of the box has been jam-fitted on to a waste piece of softwood, and the 1/4in (6mm) spindle gouge is being used to clean off and slightly concave the base.

113

Fig 17.14 shows the corner of a parting tool being used to cut in the decorative concentric lines.

Complete the box by sanding, sealing and waxing the underside.

FINISHING

Although I chose to seal and wax this example, I very often use an oil and wax finish, particularly on greasy woods such as bucote and olivewood.

For turners who wish to delve into the finer points of boxmaking I recommend Ray Key's book, *Woodturning and Design* (B.T. Batsford Ltd, 1985), which goes into great detail regarding both design and technique.

Fig 17.14 Cutting the decorative concentric lines on the base with the corner of a narrow parting tool.

Chapter 18
Egg Cups and Stand

TIME: 6 HOURS ★★★★★

As with the mug tree stand described earlier, this project is suitable for making on a production basis or as a display piece.

DESIGN CONSIDERATIONS

The design shown in Fig 18.1 is loosely based on a unit I saw in a Cotswolds antique shop and, although it was made in ebony with ivory feet and finial, the price was a staggering £1,250. I was therefore not tempted to buy, being satisfied to make a mental note of the design.

The most time-consuming (and most difficult) part of the project is the off-centre turning of the six recesses to house the base of the egg cups. For those who do not wish to go to this trouble, or those with lathes with insufficient swing (almost 16in/40.6cm required), simply bore the $\frac{1}{4}$in (6mm) holes and glue in the six pegs for the cups to locate on. This would also be the obvious method to use for production pieces.

CHOICE AND PREPARATION OF STOCK

My choice of wood was influenced by the fact that I wanted to match the species used in the mug tree stand, that is, padauk for the base and pillar and ebony for the three feet, the ovoid finial and the six locating pegs.

The base is prepared from a 10in (25.4cm) wide board and accurately planed to a uniform thickness of 1in (25mm). The pillar is from 2in (51mm) square section, and can be cut to a length of 7$\frac{1}{8}$in (181mm). For the finial a piece of ebony 2$\frac{3}{4}$in (70mm) long x 1$\frac{1}{4}$in (32mm) square section is required. The same section is required for the feet (three pieces 1$\frac{1}{2}$in/38mm

long) and for the pegs about 5in (127mm) of $\frac{1}{2}$in (13mm) square section is wanted. The egg cups are cut from 2in (51mm) square stock in lengths of 3$\frac{1}{2}$in (89mm).

ORDER OF WORK

BASE
Careful study of the drawings and photographs, particularly Figs 18.1, 18.2 and 18.3a, b and c, is essential before commencing the project. I started by making a hardboard template for the base. With a set of dividers, set out the overall circumference and then scribe a concentric circle with a 2$\frac{3}{4}$in (70mm) radius. The dividers, set on the same radius, can now be used to 'step out' six equally spaced points on this inner circle, indicating the centres of the recesses to take the base of the cups. If desired, the 1$\frac{13}{16}$in (46mm) diameter recesses can be scribed in to help visualize the proportions.

Fig 18.1 The completed project with an egg cup removed from the stand to show the recess and the ebony peg.

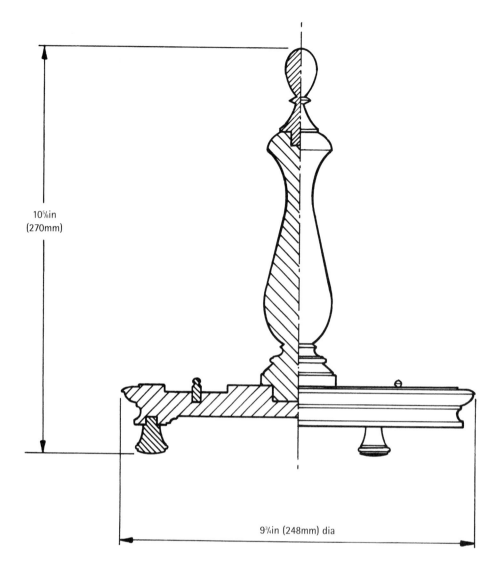

10⅝in
(270mm)

9¾in (248mm) dia

Fig 18.2 Constructional and dimensional details of the stand.

Fig 18.4 shows the template in use in setting out the underside of the base (on a piece of MDF for photographic convenience). To prevent the template moving, I think it is advisable to use two pointed awls, one in the centre and one to prick the six off-centre marks. After bandsawing the outer circle, the underside can now be prepared for your chuck.

I chose the 1in (25mm) O'Donnell jaws, and this size of chuck used in the expansion mode requires a 1⅜in (35mm) diameter recess in which to function. The seven recesses (one is also needed on the centre of the base) were bored out with a sawtooth cutter to a depth of ⅛in (3mm) on the pillar drill.

The initial mounting should be on the centre recess to enable the upper side of the

base to be trued up and also complete the whole of the edge profiling. This is achieved with a ⅜in (10mm) spindle gouge, a narrow round-nose scraper for the cove and a ⅛in (3mm) parting tool for the flats or fillets. For all of this turning, the lathe speed should be approximately 1000rpm.

Fig 18.5 (base removed from chuck) shows the underside completed to this stage. The 'mortise' in the dead centre of the face (to receive the tenon or spigot to be formed at the bottom of the pillar) can also be bored before the off-centre turning. This is achieved by using a Jacobs chuck in the tailstock, with a 1⅜in (35mm) diameter sawtooth cutter to bore a hole to a depth of ½in (13mm).

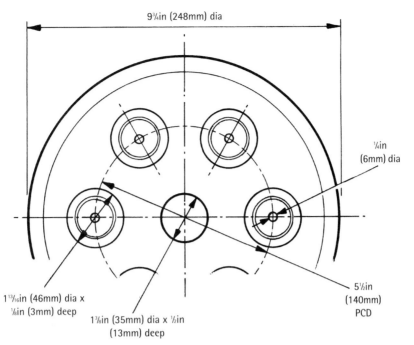

PCD: Pitch circle diameter – a circular construction line, used for spacing holes or slots.

9¾in (248mm) dia

¼in (6mm) dia

5½in (140mm) PCD

1¹³⁄₁₆in (46mm) dia x ⅛in (3mm) deep

1⅜in (35mm) dia x ½in (13mm) deep

Fig 18.3a Plan view of upper side of the base.

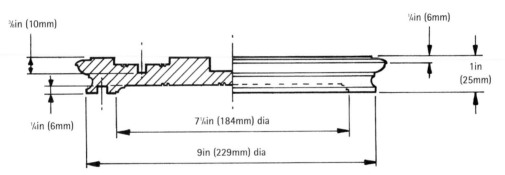

⅜in (10mm)

¼in (6mm)

¼in (6mm)

1in (25mm)

7¼in (184mm) dia

9in (229mm) dia

Fig 18.3b Section through the base.

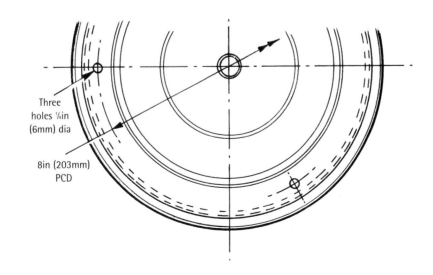

Three holes ¼in (6mm) dia

8in (203mm) PCD

Fig 18.3c Plan view of underside of base.

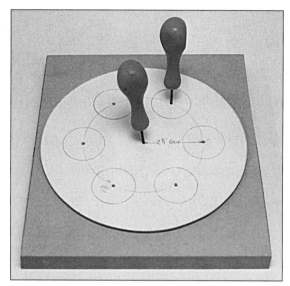

Fig 18.4 Using the hardboard template on the underside of the base (MDF for photographic convenience) to set out the hole centres for the expanding chuck. Note that two pointed awls are being used to prevent movement.

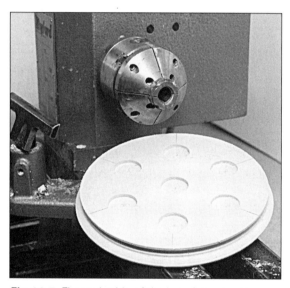

Fig 18.5 The underside of the base following the boring operation. The chuck in view will be used in the expansion mode to drive the work in each recess.

It was then necessary to swivel the headstock of my Mystro to provide sufficient 'swing' for the off-centre turning to follow. Mount the base on any one of the off-centre recesses, making sure that it is well secured. *It is absolutely vital for the lathe speed to be reduced to approximately 400rpm. It is extremely dangerous to start the lathe on too fast a speed,*

so beware. It is also important before pressing the start button to revolve the piece by hand to check that it is running free and clear of tool rests, bed bars, etc. It makes good sense also to stand out of the 'firing line' when starting up.

With the lathe running at a safe speed, the first recess can be set out with a pair of dividers set at 1$\frac{13}{16}$in (46mm) (the base of the cups will be turned to 1$\frac{3}{4}$in/44mm diameter). Some turners find it difficult to 'line up' the points, as only the point on the 'down side' of the whirling wood can safely scribe the mark. It can be made easier if a few concentric lines are made with a pencil on the wood. Fig 18.6 shows the dividers in use scribing the final recess.

Fig 18.6 Using the dividers to scribe the recess for the cup.

The recessing is perhaps most easily achieved with a $\frac{1}{4}$in (6mm) parting tool working from the centre outwards. This is followed by making use of a $\frac{1}{2}$in (13mm) skew chisel, scraper fashion, to flatten the bottom. The toe or long point of the same tool can now be used to make the two decorative lines on the bottoms and also to prick dead centre before drilling a $\frac{1}{4}$in (6mm) hole to take the ebony pegs. (These holes were drilled later on the pillar drill.) Care must be taken to ensure that all the recesses are of uniform depth, and each recess should be sanded before rechucking for the next. Fig 18.7 shows a parting tool being used to remove the bulk of the waste wood.

With all six recesses complete, the base can be reverse chucked on to the central hole (the mortise which receives the corresponding

Fig 18.7 A ¼in (6mm) parting tool being used to remove the bulk of the waste from the recess.

Fig 18.8 The completed underside of a base in MDF, clearly showing the three ¼in (6mm) holes to take the feet and the profiling after the removal of the seven recesses which served as the initial chucking.

spigot to be turned at the base of the central pillar), enabling all traces of the initial chucking method to be turned away.

Before doing this, it is advisable to set out and bore the three ¼in (6mm) holes to receive the ebony feet. The holes are located at 120° intervals at a distance of ½in (13mm) from the perimeter of the base. Fig 18.8 shows the completed underside of an MDF base.

CENTRAL PILLAR

The 7⅛in x 2in (191mm x 51mm) square stock is mounted between centres and reduced to a cylinder with a roughing-out gouge. Continue by boring a ½in (13mm) diameter hole to a depth of approximately ½in (13mm) in one end by methods described earlier. Remount (with the hole at the tailstock end) and square

off the shoulder adjacent to the hole to ensure a good fit with the ebony finial.

The stock for the finial is similarly processed, but a ½in (13mm) diameter spigot needs to be turned on one end to fit in the corresponding hole on the main stem. Dry fit them together and remount between centres, after which nearly all of the profiling can be done with gouges and chisels. Take care to ensure that the 1⅜in x ½in (35mm x 13mm) spigot that forms the joint with the base is accurately cut to give a good push fit.

Figs 18.9 and 18.10 give dimensional details of the pillar and finial respectively, and Fig 18.11 shows a ¼in (6mm) spindle gouge in use refining the cove near the base of the pillar.

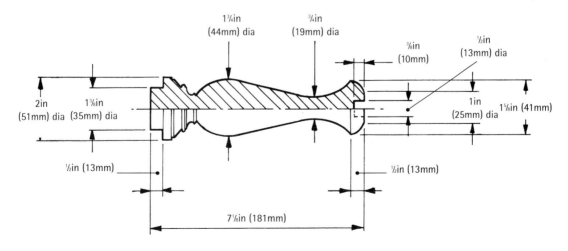

Fig 18.9 Dimensional details of the main pillar.

Fig 18.10 Dimensional details of the finial.

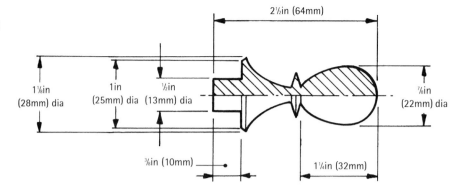

Fig 18.11 A ¼in (6mm) spindle gouge being used to refine the profile of the cove near the base of the pillar.

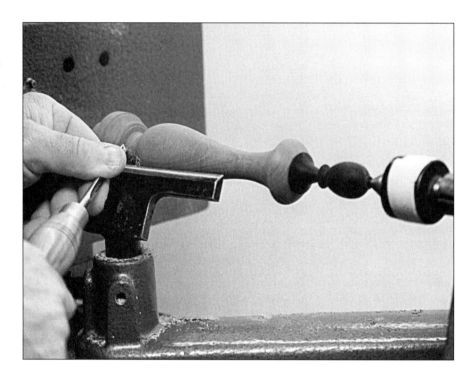

When satisfied with the overall profile, remove the finial and mount it in a softwood friction chuck (bored out with a ½in/13mm hole and described fully in the making of the finial for the mug tree in Chapter 7), and trim off the drive marks with gouge or chisel. The finial can now be glued in position.

FEET

Each 1½in (38mm) length of 1in (25mm) square stock is mounted between centres and a ¼in (6mm) diameter spigot formed at the tailstock end. This done, the bulk of the profiling can be done with a ¼in (6mm) spindle gouge and narrow parting tool. As with the finial, each part-turned foot can be reversed into a softwood friction chuck (bored out with

a ¼in/6mm hole) to enable the underside to be cleaned off and sanded. Fig 18.12 gives dimensional details of the feet.

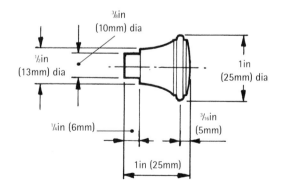

Fig 18.12 Dimensional details of the ebony feet.

EBONY PEGS

My method of producing these is to mount a 6in (152mm) length of ½in (13mm) square ebony between centres and turn it to a cylinder. I then cut it into two manageable 3in (76mm) lengths and use a Jacobs chuck in the headstock to drive each piece and turn them to the required ¼in (6mm) diameter. After working the profile at the tip of the pegs, they were parted off to the appropriate length (*see* Fig 18.13).

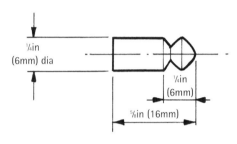

Fig 18.13 Dimensional details of the ebony pegs.

EGG CUPS

Each piece (3½in x 2in/89mm x 51mm square) is mounted between centres and a spigot worked on one end to fit in the spigot chuck. After transferring to the chuck, the piece is turned to slightly over the finished diameter of 1⅞in (47mm), followed by cleaning up of the end grain at the open end with a ¼in (6mm) spindle gouge.

The same tool can also be used to good advantage to determine the depth of each cup. A piece of masking tape is stuck on the gouge at the appropriate place (1¼in/32mm from the tip), providing an effective depth gauge as the tool is pushed down the centre of the whirling wood.

Next comes the marking out of the internal diameter of the cup. With dividers set at 1¹¹⁄₁₆in (43mm), the diameter is transferred to the wood as described earlier. The internal profile can then be fashioned with a ⅜in (10mm) spindle gouge and a side-cutting scraper.

Attention can now be given to the outside profile and it is advisable, as with any repetition turning, to prepare a marking stick from the drawing (*see* Fig 18.14). Offer the stick up to the wood, and with a pencil transfer the marks indicating the overall length, the flat area immediately adjacent to the base, and the point where the curve of the cup and the stem merge. Fig 18.15 shows the stick in use (note that all the relevant measurements have been marked on the stick).

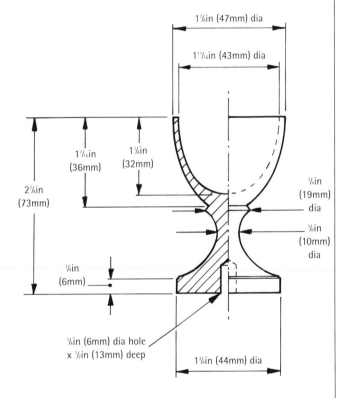

Fig 18.14 Dimensional details of the egg cup.

Fig 18.15 Making use of the marking stick to assist in the 'copy turning' process.

The sizing process is now undertaken, followed by developing the outside curve of the cup with a spindle gouge or skew chisel. The V-cut at the intersection of the cup and the stem is best done with the toe of the skew. At this stage, both the inside and outside of the cup can be sanded (and polished if wished). Leaving this until the stem is fashioned might present problems with the 'wobble factor'.

The long sweeping curve from base to cup is then blended in with the $\frac{3}{8}$in (10mm) spindle gouge. Finally, sand and polish and part off with a narrow parting tool, leaving a little extra length for cleaning off in the reverse chucking stage.

With all six cups completed, the next step is to face off the bases and bore the $\frac{1}{4}$in (6mm) holes to fit on the ebony pegs. To facilitate this operation, I made use of a piece of scrap softwood mounted on the spigot chuck. The wood was profiled to a half-egg shape to receive each cup on a push fit.

The dead centre of each base was then pricked with the toe of a skew chisel, followed by the boring of the $\frac{1}{4}$in (6mm) holes (making use of the Jacobs chuck in the tailstock).

The cup can now be completed by cleaning up the base and cutting the two concentric lines with the toe of the skew chisel as shown in Fig 18.16.

Fig 18.16 Cutting concentric lines on the base of a cup with the toe of a skew chisel.

ASSEMBLY AND FINISHING

PVA is used to glue all the component parts together, and when set I lightly hand sanded the assembled piece with 600 grit abrasive. I opted to apply the same finish as with the mug tree, that is, a sprayed-on sanding basecoat followed by wax and 'elbow grease'.

You may perhaps wish to apply the finish on the lathe as each component part is completed; this is fine as long as the areas to be glued are not coated.

Chapter 19
Square-edge Bowl

TIME: 2 HOURS ★★★★★

Although this type of bowl holds no great appeal for me, I have included one because of the numerous requests I get to demonstrate turning them at seminars, club meetings, etc.

It must be stressed at the outset that the turning of square-edge bowl blanks *can be dangerous* and should not be attempted until a high degree of proficiency and confidence has been attained.

I have never seen any written instruction on how to make one, and I shall therefore highlight the possible pitfalls and the inherent dangers of whirling square edges.

I first saw square-edge bowls demonstrated by the Australian turner Vic Wood at a Craft Supplies seminar in 1988. His method was to prepare a square blank carefully and then glue pieces of contrasting-coloured wood on all four edges. The block was subsequently bandsawn to a disc in such a manner that the original square block was left intact.

This method ensures that there are no sharp corners to catch the unwary hand, the turning being as when turning a round bowl. Once complete, what remains of the glued-on pieces can be removed with a carpenter's chisel, and the now exposed square edges can be cleaned up with a hand plane and abrasives.

Fig 19.1 Three suggested designs of square-edge bowls.

This is the method I recommend to most turners as it is much safer, and the extra time involved in the preparation and final cleaning up is well justified.

The alternative method, which is certainly more demanding in skill, nerve and technique, is to fix the square block directly on to the lathe and cut through the corners of the wood with a gouge until the desired profile is attained.

DESIGN CONSIDERATIONS

It should be understood that the larger the blank, the more demanding and dangerous the turning becomes. It makes sense, therefore, to start with a modest-sized bowl, avoiding too thin a wall thickness.

The 'swing' over the lathe bed will dictate the maximum size you can turn. It is worth noting that a 4in (102mm) square block is about 6in (152mm) from corner to corner; a 6in (152mm) square block is about 8in (203mm) and an 8in (203mm) square block is not far short of 12in (305mm).

CHOICE AND PREPARATION OF STOCK

I suggest that early efforts be restricted to inexpensive species of wood and something that also cuts easily. Sycamore, beech and ash are ideal for practice.

Fig 19.1 shows three different designs turned from the sizes just mentioned. The 4in (102mm) piece is ebony; the 6in (152mm) piece is ash, and the 8in (203mm) piece is goncalo alves. The ebony bowl is the easiest, and well suited to early attempts. The design of the ash bowl demands mastery of most of the techniques required to complete most profiles, and I have therefore chosen this. Figs 19.2, 19.3 and 19.4 illustrate cutaway sections of all three designs respectively.

The 6in (152mm) square piece was accurately centred and a pilot hole bored to facilitate the initial mounting on the screw chuck. Accurate centring is essential, otherwise an imbalance will be created, resulting in unnecessary vibration.

ORDER OF WORK

Having mounted the blank on the screw chuck, it is vital that you adjust the lathe speed to a low and safe speed *before* starting the lathe. It is good practice to revolve the work freehand to make sure that the corners clear the lathe bed and tool rest. *It is also absolutely imperative to wear a face shield.*

Stand out of the 'firing line' and start the lathe. It will be immediately apparent that the whirling square corners are difficult to see (certainly in my case). To overcome this I made a 'sighting board' which I coated with a matt finish black paint. It was necessary to cut a large, tunnel-shaped hole on the lower edge of the 'sighting board' so that it would not foul the whirling four-jaw chuck. As can be seen from Fig 19.5, the board was held in a snug-fitting slot cut in a length of 2in x 1in (51mm x 25mm) spanning the lathe bed bars. A short piece of wood screwed to the underside of the 2in x 1in (51mm x 25mm) and which is a push fit between the bed bars holds the whole thing very secure. A similar construction could be made to fit any make of lathe.

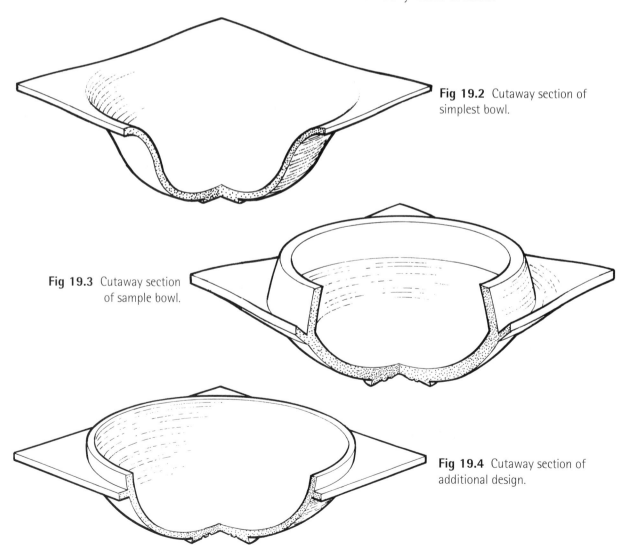

Fig 19.2 Cutaway section of simplest bowl.

Fig 19.3 Cutaway section of sample bowl.

Fig 19.4 Cutaway section of additional design.

Now to the actual making of the bowl. First of all, with the lathe stationary, draw a bold pencil line along one edge of the blank a distance of ⅝in (16mm) from the face nearest the headstock. This mark can easily be seen when the wood is spinning and serves to indicate the limit of the outside curve. Set out the 1½in (38mm) diameter spigot at the base of the bowl with a pair of dividers, and cut to a depth of a full ⅛in (3mm) with a parting tool and skew chisel.

The ogee profile can now be fashioned with a bowl gouge, stopping the cuts just short of the bold pencil mark on the edge. A skew chisel used scraper fashion can be used to blend in the intersection of the slightly dovetailed spigot and the commencement of the outside curve.

At this stage, stop the lathe and draw in a bold pencil mark on the outside curve at a distance of ⁵⁄₁₆in (8mm) from the outside edge. This line indicates where a slight step is cut into the profile. This step also acts as an aiming point when the bowl is reverse chucked so as to ensure that the profile is continuous and flowing through the square edge.

Fig 19.5 shows this line very clearly, and Fig 19.6 shows a skew chisel being used to create the step. Light refining cuts to blend in the profile can now be taken with a ¼in (6mm) bowl gouge as shown in Fig 19.7. Scrapers can be used to further refine the outside profile, but great care must be taken near the square edges.

An optional way of finishing the base of the spigot is to cut the profile shown in Fig 19.8. I chose to do this by using a ¼in (6mm) spindle gouge to fashion the profile, as shown in Fig 19.9.

Fig 19.6 The step being cut with the toe of the skew chisel.

Fig 19.5 The blank has been mounted on a screw chuck and the initial profiling has been completed. A pencil mark indicates where a step is to be cut to ensure profile continuity through the square edge. Note how the black 'sighting board' highlights the whirling corners.

Fig 19.7 Refining the outside profile with a ¼in (6mm) bowl gouge.

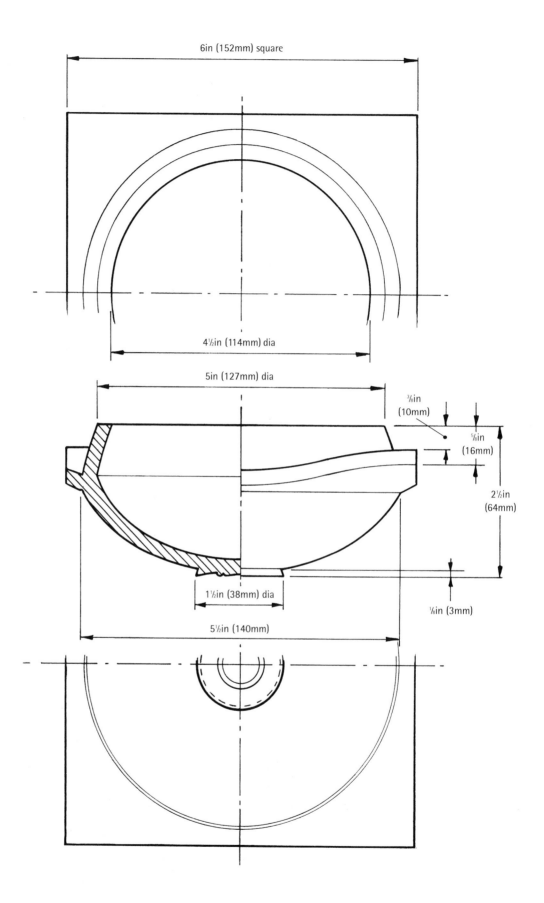

6in (152mm) square

4½in (114mm) dia

5in (127mm) dia

⅜in (10mm)

⅝in (16mm)

2½in (64mm)

1½in (38mm) dia

⅛in (3mm)

5½in (140mm)

Fig 19.8 Dimensional details of the sample bowl.

After sanding (more on this later) and applying your choice of finish, the bowl can be reverse chucked, in this case on to the 1½in (38mm) spigot chuck.

Before commencing the turning, it is necessary to plane off the pencil mark on the edge of the blank (⅝in/16mm from the edge), otherwise it tends to throw your focus from the outside profile you will be attempting to follow when shaping the top of the bowl.

Continue by trueing up the face of the bowl with a ⅜in (10mm) bowl gouge, followed by pencilling in the three concentric lines shown in Figs 19.8 and 19.10. The outside mark is 5/16in (8mm) in from the edge of the bowl (to line up with the outside profile). The middle line indicates the limit of the taper, and the other mark is the required wall thickness.

Note also in Fig 19.10 that another siting board has been slotted on to the cross-piece spanning the bed bars to assist in 'viewing' the whirling square corners.

Now to the most demanding part of the cutting, that is, from the outside square edge into the 'solid' wood. I find that a ⅜in (10mm) bowl gouge, ground with a long bevel and with the wings swept well back, makes for easier entry and also facilitates the cutting of the intersection where the square edge and bowl wall merge (*see* Fig 19.11).

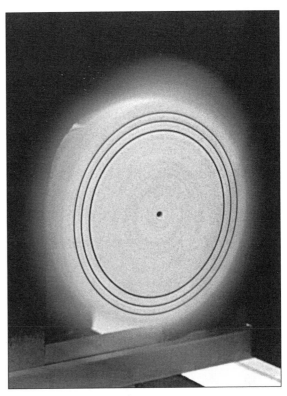

Fig 19.10 The three concentric lines have been pencilled in to indicate wall thickness and the degree of taper. Note that a second sighting board has been fixed at the back of the lathe to provide clear viewing from the front.

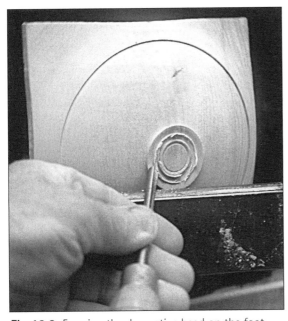

Fig 19.9 Forming the decorative bead on the foot.

Fig 19.11 Using a long-bevelled ⅜in (10mm) bowl gouge to cut into the square.

Needless to say, the bevel of the gouge must be lined up with the profile on the underside of the bowl and swung in an arc if a parallel rim is to be effected. It will also be necessary to make alternative cuts from the outside line on the face of the bowl (at right angles to the face) so as to merge with the rim profile.

To effect the tapered profile on the upper bowl wall, cut back to the next pencil line, lining up the bevel of the gouge so that the taper blends into the previously created intersection of rim and wall (*see* Fig 19.12).

The crispness of this intersection can be improved by using an acutely ground ½in (13mm) skew chisel, used scraper fashion as shown in Fig 19.13.

Some of the above procedures may sound complicated, but careful study of the photographs should clarify the procedures.

Please note that if scrapers are used to remove gouge marks on the rim cut so far (and I used one) extreme care must be taken, especially near the square edges.

Fig 19.12 Using the same tool to form the tapered wall.

Fig 19.13 Using an acutely ground skew chisel to cut a crisp intersection.

thickness as indicated by the last pencil mark on the face should be about ¼in (6mm). If preferred, the inside can be a sweeping curve which is quite easy to achieve. I chose to cut the inside profile as parallel as I could to the outside profile, as shown in Fig 19.8.

Most of the waste wood is removed with the ¼in (6mm) bowl gouge (*see* Fig 19.15), but I had to resort to scrapers to form the upper inside wall and intersection with the curved lower portion. A careful study of Fig 19.16 should assist greatly with the direction of gouge cuts in the interests of safety and clean cutting.

Fig 19.14 View from front of the lathe showing the effectiveness of the sighting boards.

Fig 19.14 is a view from the front of the lathe, and shows the effectiveness of the black siting boards in highlighting the profile and whirling square edges.

Now for the easiest part of the bowl, that is, the gouging out of the centre. The wall

Fig 19.15 Removing the bulk of the inside with a bowl gouge. Note the cone of wood in the centre which has been deliberately left to provide maximum stability while cutting the upper bowl wall.

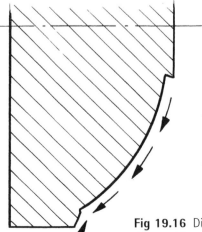

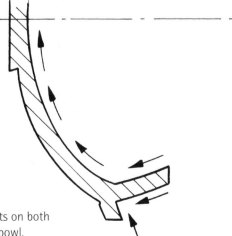

Fig 19.16 Direction of gouge cuts on both the outside and the inside of the bowl.

FINISHING

There is a tendency to relax when all the tooling has been done on any form of woodturning, and sanding is regarded as just a matter of course. *Be warned* that the highest level of concentration is required when sanding this type of work or you may finish up with smashed knuckles.

Thread the paper and not your fingers into the corners and hold the paper lightly. It is dangerous to try to sand too close to the square edges. Be prepared to spend some time hand sanding (with the lathe stationary) the corners, and all four edges will need cleaning up with a hand plane followed by sanding.

My choice of finish for this bowl was two coats of brush-on sanding sealer, cut back with 600 grit wet or dry paper, and finally a coat of wax buffed up to a pleasing sheen (*see* Fig 19.17).

Final thoughts on this particular project are to emphasize again the need to be a competent and experienced turner before tackling this method of producing square-edge bowls. Additionally, even the most experienced turner needs to maintain a maximum level of concentration to avoid being rendered *hors de combat*.

Fig 19.17 Applying the final coat of wax.

Chapter 20
Pocket Watch Stand

TIME: 2¾ HOURS ★★★★★

Although not as popular as they were many years ago, pocket watches still form a prominent display in the windows of many jeweller's shops. It follows, therefore, that both jewellers and pocket watch owners may well be tempted to buy attractively made stands on which to display them.

Such stands were extremely popular in Victorian times, and the design of this example is similar to a stand I saw at an antique fair.

DESIGN CONSIDERATIONS

The stand needs to be stable without looking bulky. Some were made with the two pillars turned on a baluster profile, but for me the tapered style used in the example looks better. I also prefer the arch to be of square section and not the round-section arch seen on many.

Many well-turned stands I have seen displayed at craft fairs and the like have been completely ruined by the fitting of a cheap brass-plated cup hook on which the watch is suspended. A well-made, attractive stand requires an equally attractive, solid brass hook.

To add to the neatness of the presentation, I have turned a shallow hemisphere in the upper face of the base, into which the detached watch chain can nestle unobtrusively. This, I feel, looks much nicer than allowing the chain to cascade untidily as it does when still attached to the watch.

To be a success, the construction calls for precise boring, turning and jointing.

CHOICE AND PREPARATION OF STOCK

A project like this demands the use of some nice, exotic wood, and most types of rosewood are eminently suitable. Contrasting-coloured woods can also look very appealing, and for the completed example I chose padauk for the base and arch and ebony for the pillars and finial.

Fig 20.1 shows a completed stand.

The cutting list for the project is as follows: base, 1in (25mm) stock x 4¼in (108mm) diameter; arch, ⅜in (10mm) stock x 3¼in (82mm) diameter; pillars, ⅝in (16mm) square stock x 4¼in (108mm) long, and the finial from the same section x 2½in (64mm) long.

Fig 20.1 A completed stand in padauk and ebony.

ORDER OF WORK

Careful study of the drawings and the
photographs is essential before you begin work.

Fig 20.2 is a cutaway drawing of the stand
to show constructional details, and Fig 20.3
shows a part section of the stand and the
overall height.

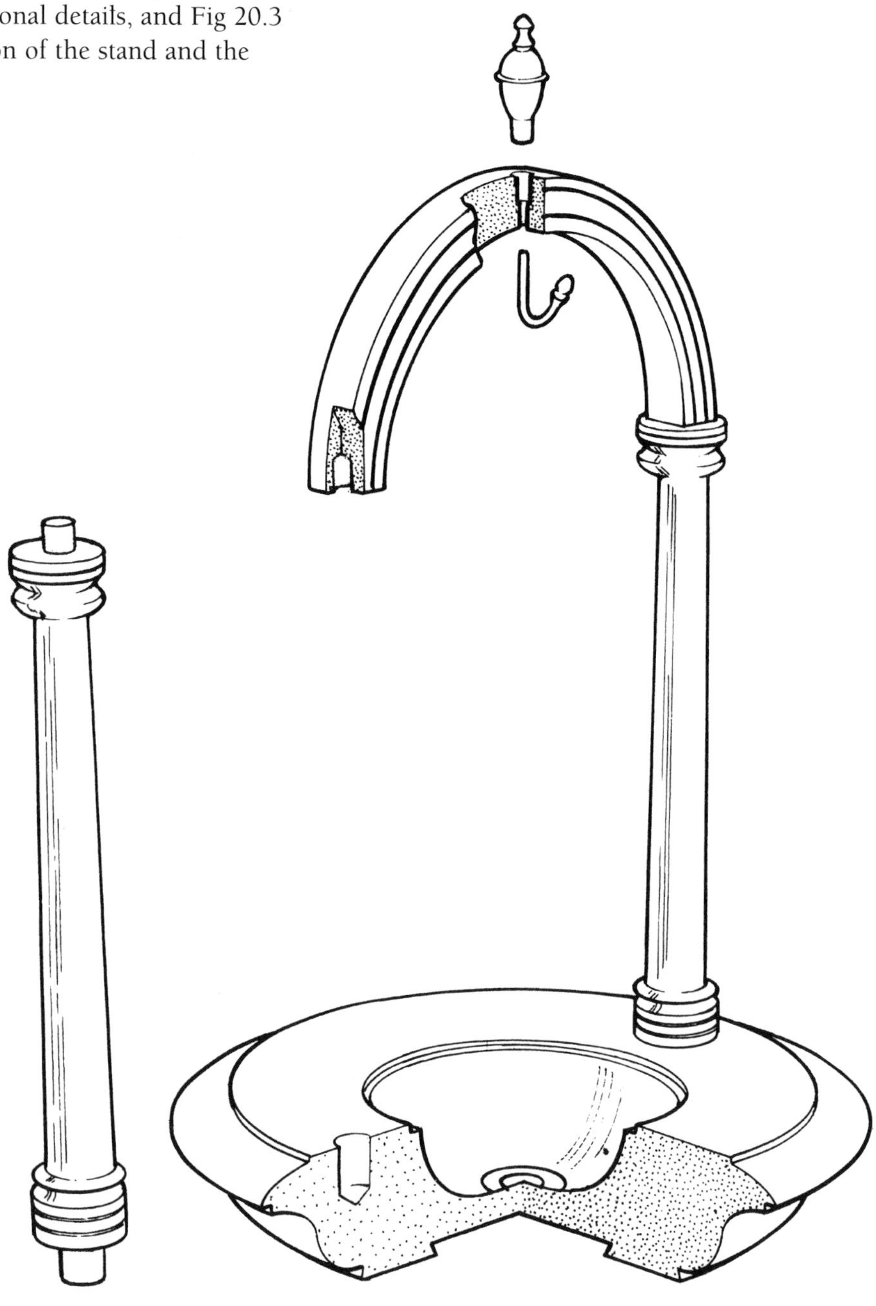

Fig 20.2 Constructional details with cutaway section.

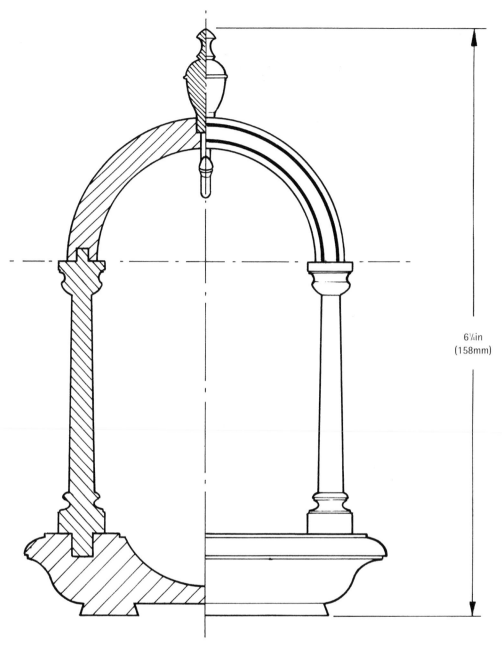

6¼in
(158mm)

Fig 20.3 Part section through stand.

BASE

Commence by making the base (Fig 20.4 provides dimensional details). Initial fixing is made to the intended upper side of the base by means of a screw chuck. I found it necessary to limit the length of the screw to ⅜in (10mm) by using plywood packers between the stock and the face of the chuck. (The screw hole will subsequently be turned away after the reverse-chucking process – too deep a screw hole would need an unnecessary amount of wood to be removed.)

After facing off the underside with a ⅜in (10mm) spindle gouge, cut a shallow recess of 1⅜in (35mm) diameter to accept your smallest expanding jaws (*see* Fig 20.5). The underside is then sanded, followed by two coats of sealer and a final application of paste wax.

After reverse chucking, continue by accurately levelling the face and then pencil a 2¾in (70mm) diameter line on the whirling wood (the hole centres measurement for the pillars). Remove the base from the chuck and carefully locate two ⅜in (10mm) diameter

133

Fig 20.4 Dimensional details of the base.

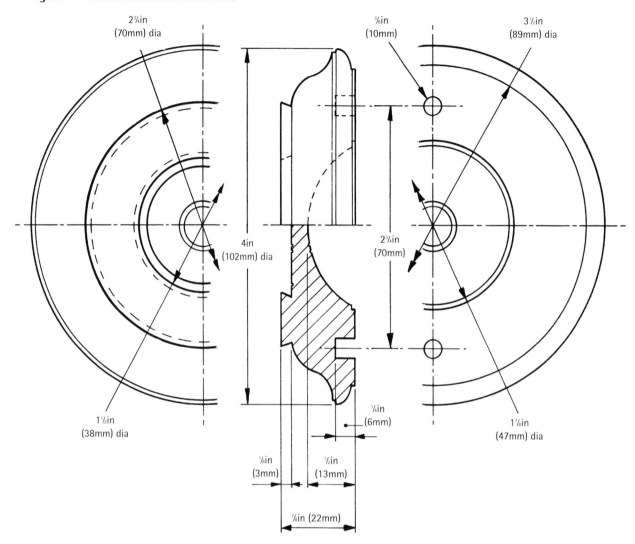

2¾in
(70mm) dia

⅜in
(10mm)

3½in
(89mm) dia

4in
(102mm) dia

2¾in
(70mm)

1½in
(38mm) dia

¼in
(6mm)

1⅞in
(47mm) dia

⅛in
(3mm)

½in
(13mm)

⅞in (22mm)

Fig 20.5 The base has been mounted on a screw chuck, enabling the shallow recess to be formed (on the intended underside) to accommodate the expanding chuck when reversed.

holes at 180° intervals, bored on the pillar drill to a depth of ¼in (6mm).

Remount the base on the chuck and cut away the central 1⅞in x ⁷⁄₁₆in (47mm x 11mm) hemisphere with a ⅜in (10mm) spindle gouge and round-nose scraper (thus removing the screw hole). For added decoration cut in two concentric lines on its bottom with the toe of the skew chisel (*see* Fig 20.6).

Now for the profiling of the edge of the base, which is achieved with the same gouge, parting tool and scraper. The sanding, sealing and waxing process can now be repeated, but care must be taken not to get wax in the two holes or it will render the glue useless. Fig 20.7 shows a completed and polished base.

134

Fig 20.6 The base has been reverse chucked and the shallow hemisphere formed with gouge and scraper. The toe of the skew is seen being used to cut the two concentric lines at the bottom of the curve.

Fig 20.7 A completed base.

ARCH

Fig 20.8 gives the dimensional details. The initial mounting is again made on the screw chuck with the plywood packers employed between stock and chuck to prevent damage to

the tool when parting through. The finished diameter of 3⅛in (79mm) is worked and the face trued up. At a distance of ⁵⁄₁₆in (8mm) from the edge a pencil line is then struck on the face of the whirling wood, indicating the location of the parting cut.

Before parting all the way through, you will need to cut in the two concentric lines on the

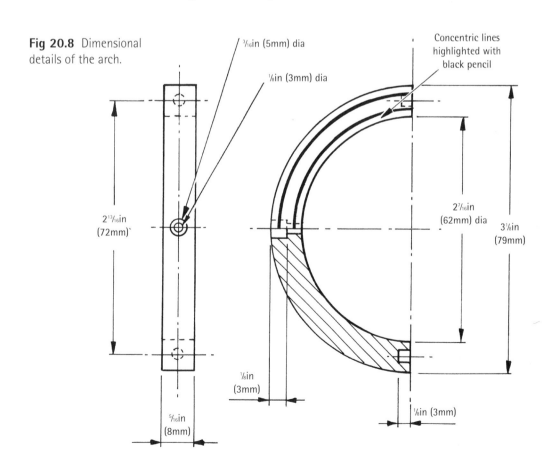

Fig 20.8 Dimensional details of the arch.

³⁄₁₆in (5mm) dia

⅛in (3mm) dia

Concentric lines highlighted with black pencil

2¹³⁄₁₆in (72mm)

2⁷⁄₁₆in (62mm) dia

3⅛in (79mm)

⅛in (3mm)

⅛in (3mm)

⁵⁄₁₆in (8mm)

135

Fig 20.9 The stock for the arch has been mounted on a screw chuck, dimensioned, and the exposed areas sanded and polished. A narrow parting tool is being used to cut through the stock. Note that a plywood packer has been inserted between the chuck and the stock to prevent the tool edge being damaged.

face with the corner of a narrow parting tool. These lines can be highlighted to give the appearance of ebony inlay by simply holding the point of a pencil in the grooves as the stock rotates. The sanding and polishing process on the exposed faces also needs to be done before parting through.

Fig 20.9 shows the parting-through process almost completed. Note that it is advisable to part through the last ⅛in (3mm) of thickness well into the wastewood side. In the event of any grain 'break-out', it can be cleaned off after reverse chucking.

Fig 20.10 The arch has been reverse chucked on a softwood jam chuck to facilitate the turning of the other side. A parting tool is being used to cut the two concentric lines on the face. These lines can be highlighted with a black pencil if necessary. Note the two inked-in marks on the jam chuck at 180° intervals (accurately located by means of the inbuilt dividing head). These greatly assist in the lining up of the grain and the sawing process.

To facilitate the reverse chucking, prepare a softwood jam chuck and carefully cut a recess into it to receive the partially completed arch on a gentle push fit. This enables you to face off to the finished width and thickness. Decorate the face in an identical fashion to the other side, and also sand and polish (*see* Fig 20.10).

The dividing head on my Mystro was used to good effect to ink in two marks on the softwood chuck at intervals of 180° (these can also be clearly seen on Fig 20.10). They are invaluable in lining up the grain to the best effect, and also ensure the accurate sawing of the arch into two equal sections (a fine-toothed saw is essential for this – *see* Fig 20.11).

The ends of the arch are then accurately centred and drilled to the appropriate depth

Fig 20.11 A fine-toothed saw being used to cut the arch in two, the inked-in lines on the jam-fit chuck serving as accurate guides.

Fig 20.12 Method of boring the ⅛in (3mm) diameter holes in the ends of the arch. Note the fibreboard placed between the metal jaws and the arch to prevent crushing.

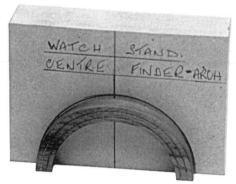

Fig 20.13 Simple jig in MDF serving as a centre finder.

with a ⅛in (3mm) drill to receive the spigots to be turned on the pillars. Fig 20.12 shows this process.

It is also necessary to drill a ³⁄₁₆in (5mm) hole to a depth of ⅛in (3mm) halfway in the centre of the arch to accommodate the spigot on the base of the finial, and also a ⅛in (3mm) hole to receive the brass hook in the bottom half. Accuracy is vital, and a simple jig similar to that shown in Fig 20.13 assists greatly in finding the centre of the arch. I find it best to drill the ⅛in (3mm) hole from the top all the way through the arch, followed by enlarging the top half with the ³⁄₁₆in (5mm) drill afterwards.

PILLARS

Dimensional details are shown in Fig 20.14.

The square-section stock is mounted directly into your smallest spigot chuck, and the tailstock live centre is then engaged to provide very light support. After the roughing-down process to slightly over the finished diameter of ½in (13mm), use a marking stick prepared from the drawings to set out the shoulders and design features on the whirling wood (*see* Fig 20.15).

The sizing-in of the spigots at each end is carefully done with the aid of vernier calipers. Note that the spigot at the tailstock end is only ⅛in (3mm) diameter, hence the need for the stock to be driven in a spigot chuck with only

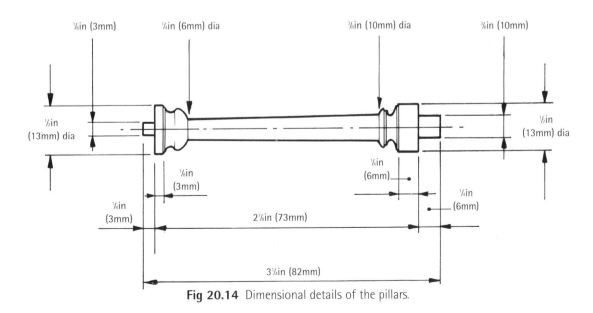

Fig 20.14 Dimensional details of the pillars.

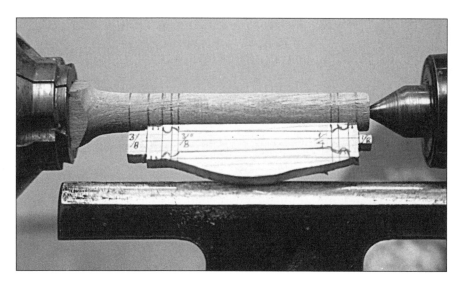

Fig 20.15 A marking stick has been prepared and has been used to mark out the salient points on the roughed-down pillar blank.

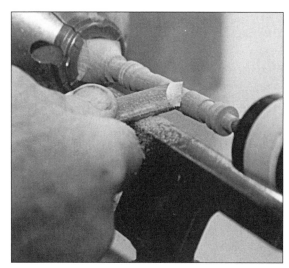

Fig 20.16 A ¹⁄₂in (13mm) skew chisel being used to work the taper on a pillar.

very light support from the tailstock (other than very light tailstock pressure would split the spigot).

Fig 20.16 shows the taper on the pillar being worked with a small oval skew chisel. Each pillar can be sanded, sealed and waxed on the lathe.

FINIAL

Dimensional details are shown in Fig 20.17.

Again, the square section stock is mounted straight into the chuck and the profile worked with a small spindle gouge and parting tool (see Fig 20.18). The ³⁄₁₆in (5mm) diameter spigot must be exactly sized to provide a gentle push fit into the corresponding hole in the top of the arch.

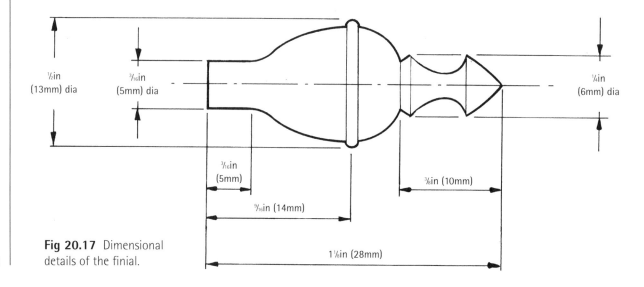

Fig 20.17 Dimensional details of the finial.

½in (13mm) dia ³⁄₁₆in (5mm) dia ¼in (6mm) dia ³⁄₁₆in (5mm) ⁹⁄₁₆in (14mm) ³⁄₈in (10mm) 1⅛in (28mm)

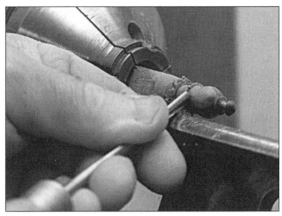

Fig 20.18 The finial blank has been mounted directly into the spigot chuck and the profiling is being undertaken with a small spindle gouge.

BRASS HOOK

The hooks I use are hand-turned from $\frac{1}{8}$in (3mm) brass rod and bent to shape on a simple jig by David Francis, a friend of mine. For those turners who do not wish to go to the trouble of making their own hooks, small and neat solid brass ones are available from good quality hardware stores.

ASSEMBLY

Use PVA glue for all the joints, but to secure the brass hook in the $\frac{1}{8}$in (3mm) hole use a drop of superglue. The stand is gripped in a vice with foam rubber pads inserted between jaws and wood to prevent damage. Apply *very light pressure* to pull the component parts together, and leave clamped until the glue has dried off.

FINISHING

Each component part can be sanded and polished before removing from the lathe, but care must be taken not to coat the areas to be glued.

Chapter 21
Pair of Matching Urns

TIME: 6 HOURS ★★★★★

A visit to one of the stately homes of England can be an inspiration to any woodturner, with classical profiles in evidence on staircases, furniture, pottery, ceramics and glass. The matching urns in the example are similar to a pair I saw adorning a beautiful marble fireplace in a large country house in my native Derbyshire. Although they are intended to be purely ornamental, they may, of course, be used to store small items.

DESIGN CONSIDERATIONS

Many wooden urns I have seen were made with the wall thickness of the lid almost twice that of the walls on the main body. I think it best to make them of equal thickness so that any tendency for the stock to move or distort is balanced.

Ideally, I should have preferred to make the urns in one species of exotic wood, but obtaining it in the required dimensions is extremely difficult. I therefore decided to use two contrasting-coloured timbers: wych elm for the cup, and ebony for the base, stem and finial.

Fig 21.1 The completed urns. The lid has been removed from one urn to highlight the contrasting ebony spigots.

One problem with jointing the component parts together is that extra thickness of wood is required at the top of the lid (to take the spigot turned on the bottom of the finial) and also at the bottom of the main body (to take the spigot turned on the top end of the stem).

To overcome this, I decided to make these two particular joints a feature. Rather than bore 'blind' holes for these two joints I opted to bore through, thus allowing the contrasting-coloured ebony spigots to be exposed. I think it adds interest and provides a pleasant surprise when the lid is removed. Fig 21.1 shows the samples, one having had the lid removed to highlight the ebony spigots.

CHOICE AND PREPARATION OF STOCK

Urns, boxes, vases with lids, etc. are best made from end-grained timber, preferably hard and close grained. As mentioned earlier, obtaining stock of the thickness required for the cup section of this project is difficult. You may well, therefore, have to make use of a species such as elm, sycamore or mahogany, and possibly consider a contrasting-coloured timber for the other component parts as I did.

Whatever your choice, it must be bone dry. Ideally, the stock should have been roughed down, partly hollowed and allowed to dry in similar conditions to those in which it will eventually be sited.

The cutting list for a single urn is as follows: main body, 4½in (114mm) square section x 5½in (140mm) long end-grain elm; finial, 2in (51mm) square section x 3in (76mm) long end-grain ebony; stem, 2in (51mm) square section x 4in (102mm) long ebony; plinth, 3in (76mm) square section x 1⅛in (28mm) long end-grain ebony.

ORDER OF WORK

To succeed with this project a strict order of work and chronological rechucking must be observed. Note that, for photographic convenience, pine and padauk have been used in the sequence shots. Fig 21.2 provides a three-dimensional view of the urn, and Fig 21.3

shows a part section and overall height. Again, careful study of the drawings is essential.

The stock for the main body is mounted between centres, reduced to a cylinder, and a spigot formed at each end to suit your choice of chuck. The depth of the lid ($1\frac{7}{8}$in/47mm) is pencilled in (*see* Fig 21.4). The parting through can be done on the lathe or on the bandsaw.

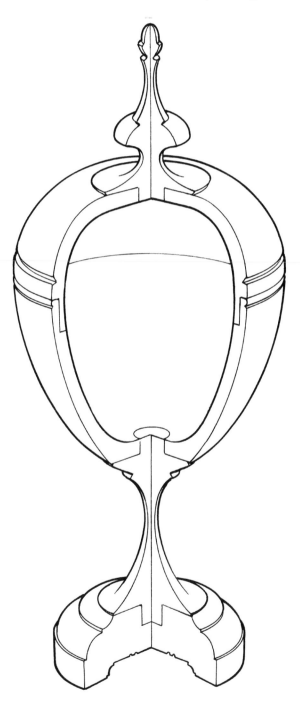

Fig 21.2 Three-dimensional view of the urn.

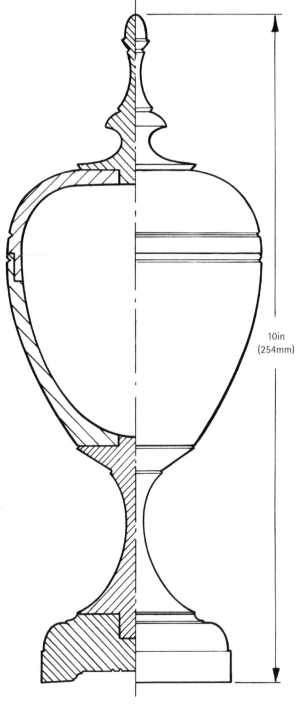

10in
(254mm)

Fig 21.3 Part section and overall height of urn.

141

Fig 21.4 The main body mounted between centres and a spigot formed at both ends to suit your preferred chuck. The length of the lid has also been marked in.

Transfer the lid section to the spigot chuck, true up the side and end grain, and form the spigot for the lid fit – about $^3/_{16}$in (5mm) deep x $^3/_8$in (10mm) wide. The inside of the lid can now be *partially* excavated to a depth of about $1^1/_8$in (28mm). Fig 21.5 provides dimensional

details of the lid, and Fig 21.6 shows a spindle gouge employed in the hollowing process. No sanding is required at this stage.

Transfer the main body to the chuck, true it up, and form the rebate to take the spigot on the lid on a drive fit. *Partial* hollowing to a

Fig 21.6 The lid has been parted off and transferred to the chuck. The spigot for the lid fit has been formed with a parting tool, and a spindle gouge is being employed to partially hollow out the inside.

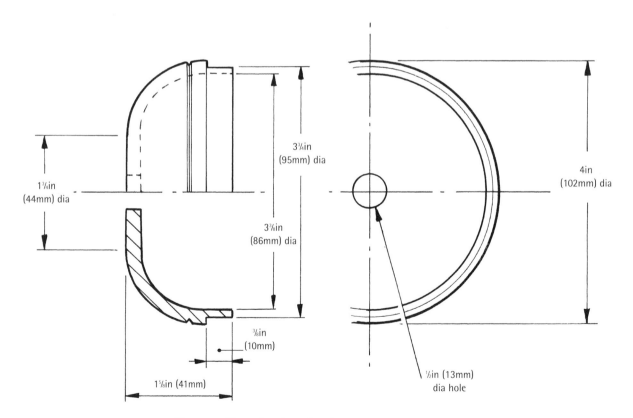

$3^3/_4$in (95mm) dia

$1^3/_4$in (44mm) dia

$3^3/_8$in (86mm) dia

$^3/_8$in (10mm)

$1^5/_8$in (41mm)

4in (102mm) dia

$^1/_2$in (13mm) dia hole

Fig 21.5 Dimensional details of the lid.

Fig 21.7 Dimensional details of the main body.

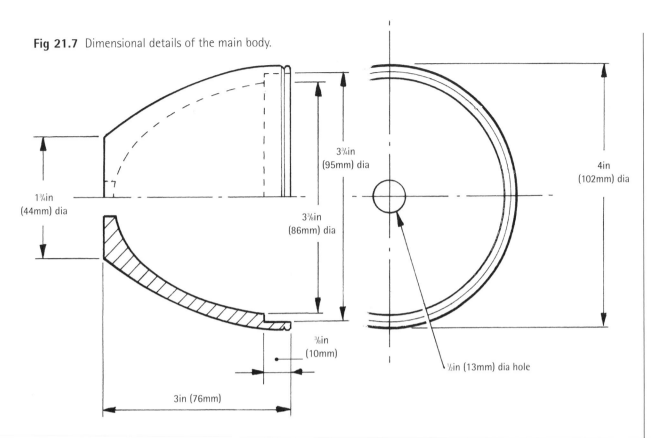

1¾in (44mm) dia

3¾in (95mm) dia

3⅜in (86mm) dia

4in (102mm) dia

⅜in (10mm)

3in (76mm)

½in (13mm) dia hole

depth of about 2in (51mm) can now be done. Fig 21.7 provides dimensional details of the main body, and Fig 21.8 shows the lid about to be test-fitted.

Fit the lid and bring up the tailstock for support. The length of the main body (3in/76mm) can now be pencilled on the whirling wood and sized in to a depth of 1¾in (44mm) (in the waste side). The length of the

lid (1⅜in/35mm from the joint) can be pencilled in similarly and parted right off.

By means of a drill bit or Jacobs chuck secured in the tailstock, bore a ½in (13mm) hole in the top of the lid and also scribe a pencil line on a 1¾in (44mm) diameter. This area will be left flat to form the joint with the finial and also limit the extent of the outside curve, as will the similar sizing at the base of

Fig 21.8 The main body has been mounted on the chuck. The rebate forming the fit with the lid has been formed with a parting tool, and the inside has been partially hollowed. The lid is shown about to be offered up to test the fit.

143

Fig 21.9 The lid has been jam-fitted to the main body, enabling the ½in (13mm) hole to be bored in the lid while on the lathe. A spindle gouge is being used to blend in the curve down to the flat area (1¾in/44mm diameter line) which forms the joint with the finial base.

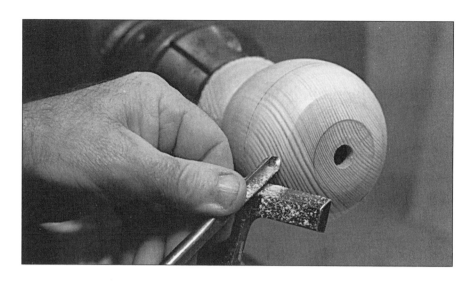

Fig 21.10 A ½in x ½in (13mm x 13mm) spigot has been formed on the stock for the finial and the lid jam-fitted to it, enabling the inside to be refined.

the main body. Fig 21.9 shows a spindle gouge being used to refine the outside curve down to the pencil line. Note that it is advisable to bring up the tailstock live centre to support the piece while shaping. It has been taken away in Fig 21.9 in order to expose the hole for clarity.

Prepare the stock intended for the finial to suit your choice of chuck. Form a spigot at the open end ½in x ½in (13mm x 13mm) and jam the lid on to it. Do not glue at this stage.

Now turn the inside to an even wall thickness to match the outside curve. Sand and polish the inside of the lid. Fig 21.10 shows the inside before the sanding process.

Remount the main body, fit the lid, and profile the finial with a small spindle gouge as shown in Fig 21.11. Dimensional details of the finial are shown in Fig 21.12.

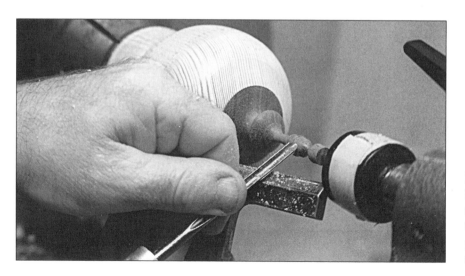

Fig 21.11 The main body has been rechucked and the lid fitted, and the finial is shown being profiled with a small spindle gouge.

Fig 21.12 Dimensional details of the finial.

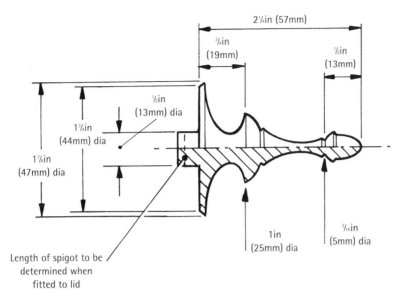

2¼in (57mm)

¾in (19mm)

½in (13mm)

½in (13mm) dia

1¾in (44mm) dia

1⅞in (47mm) dia

1in (25mm) dia

³⁄₁₆in (5mm) dia

Length of spigot to be determined when fitted to lid

Part off the main body and reverse chuck it on a softwood jam fit. The Jacobs chuck fixed in the tailstock can now be used to facilitate the boring of the ½in (13mm) hole in the base of the main body. Fig 21.13 shows the process to this stage and a small spindle gouge being used to slightly concave the base to provide a good fit with the stem.

Prepare the stock for the stem between centres, forming a ½in x ½in (13mm x 13mm) spigot at both ends to form the joints with the main body and plinth respectively. Fig 21.14 shows a parting tool and caliper being used for

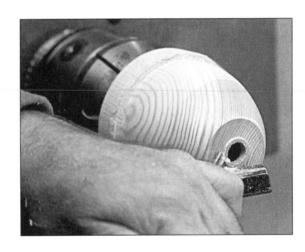

Fig 21.13 The main body has been parted off and jam-fitted to scrap softwood, enabling the ½in (13mm) hole to be bored. A spindle gouge is being used to concave slightly the area forming the joint with the stem.

Fig 21.14 The spigots on the stem being sized to fit the corresponding holes on the cup and plinth.

145

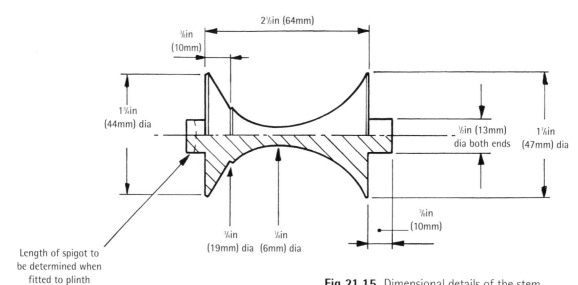

Fig 21.15 Dimensional details of the stem.

the sizing. Dimensional details of the stem are shown in Fig 21.15.

Prepare the plinth for your choice of chuck. I bored a 1⅜in (35mm) hole in the underside to accept my smallest expanding chuck. The ½in (13mm) hole can now be bored in the upper side and the pillar fixed to it (with

tailstock support) so that the profiles can be blended in between plinth and stem. Fig 21.16 gives dimensional details of the plinth, and Fig 21.17 shows the stem about to be offered up to test the fit.

Glue the main body to the stem and trim the inside of the cup to your satisfaction. Sand

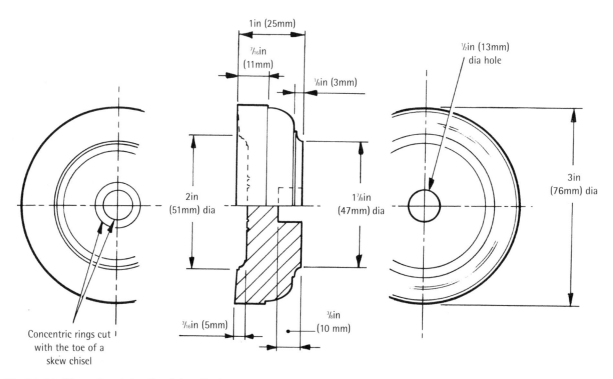

Fig 21.16 Dimensional details of the plinth.

Fig 21.17 The hole in the plinth has been bored on the lathe, and the stem is being offered up to test the fit.

Fig 21.18 Some of the component parts have been jam-fitted together so that the inside and spigot can be blended in.

and polish the inside. (Note that the stem is not glued to the plinth yet.) Fig 21.18 shows the inside ready for cleaning up, the spigot clearly visible and protruding.

With the plinth still chucked, assemble the whole piece and mark in and form the

decorative bead and V-cut adjacent to the lid and main body. Fig 21.19 shows the assembled piece before this process.

Use the ½in (13mm) hole in the upper side of the plinth to reverse chuck it on a softwood spigot. The initial means of chucking can then

Fig 21.19 All the component parts being driven between centres before forming the bead and V-cut adjacent to the joint between lid and main body.

Fig 21.20 The ½in (13mm) hole in the upper side of the plinth has been used to rechuck it so that the underside can be cleaned off and profiled with a spindle gouge.

be removed and profiled, as shown in the drawings. Fig 21.20 shows this being done with a ¼in (6mm) spindle gouge.

The unglued finial can be mounted again on a softwood chuck with a ½in (13mm) hole bored in it to receive the spigot on a push fit. This is to enable the completion of the very tip.

ASSEMBLY

The component parts can now be glued together. If the finial is removed and left until last, the lathe (with the tailstock engaged in the ½in/13mm hole at the top of the lid) can be used to clamp the piece together until the glue has set. To prevent damage to the profiled underside of the plinth a piece of scrap plywood should be inserted between the drive centre and the plinth during this gluing-up operation. I used PVA.

Finally, glue in the finial with superglue.

FINISHING

Your choice of finish can be applied as the component parts are made, or alternatively the whole piece can be oiled and waxed after completion. All you have to do now is make another identical urn, and each lid should fit both cups!

Chapter 22
Goblets

TIME: 2¼ HOURS ★★★★★

These have been produced by woodturners for hundreds of years and numerous shapes and sizes have evolved. Drinking vessels also provide the opportunity for more artistic urges to be fulfilled, with attention being paid to design and aesthetic appeal as well as to function.

DESIGN CONSIDERATIONS

Sizes and designs are almost endless, and Fig 22.1 shows several shapes that you may wish to copy. The long-stemmed goblets (the tallest is 16in/40.6cm) are purely ornamental, as are the smallest (1in/25mm tall) and the natural-edge yew wood goblet with the 'anchor' and captive rings.

The remaining two could have been classed as functional if they had not been coated with a cellulose-based finish (more on finishing later).

I decided to explain how I went about making two of the examples shown: the ebony long-stemmed goblet (12in/30.5cm tall) and the natural-edged yew wood goblet with captive rings. In my opinion, captive rings are shown to their best effect when 'anchored' in the middle of the stem rather than allowed to rest untidily on the base.

Both are very popular demonstration pieces, and the longer of the two provides the opportunity to make use of the steady shown in Chapter 2.

It must be appreciated that the longer and thinner the stem, the greater the demand on the technical skills of the turner, steady or no steady. For this reason, your early efforts should be restricted to about 6in (152mm) or 7in (178mm) overall. I prefer to see a tapered stem rather like a tree trunk, with the thinnest section immediately under the cup, and most of my goblets are shaped in this way.

CHOICE AND PREPARATION OF STOCK

LONG-STEMMED GOBLET

It is absolutely vital for the chosen species to be sound and straight grained – any twisted grain in the stem will inevitably lead to a broken goblet. Limb wood such as yew is fine, but species with a pronounced pith, such as sycamore, should be avoided.

My chosen species for the example was ebony. This is not the easiest of woods to cut to a thin stem, as it is very brittle, but I managed to get away with it. The stock required is a piece of 2½in (64mm) square section x 12in (305mm) long. (For photographic convenience I have used Scots pine in the sequence

Fig 22.1 Various designs of goblets.

149

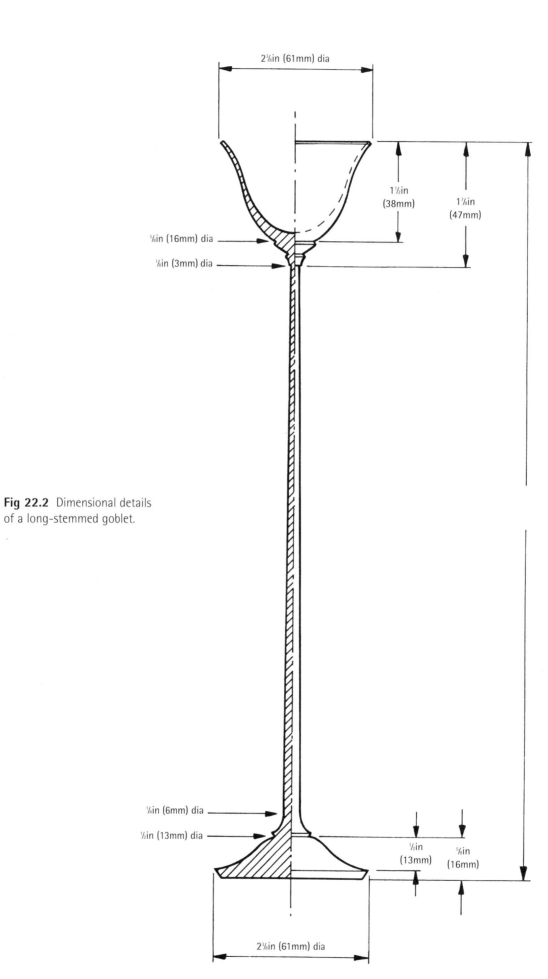

2⅜in (61mm) dia

1½in
(38mm)

1⅞in
(47mm)

⅝in (16mm) dia

⅛in (3mm) dia

Fig 22.2 Dimensional details
of a long-stemmed goblet.

¼in (6mm) dia

½in (13mm) dia

½in
(13mm)

⅝in
(16mm)

2⅜in (61mm) dia

Fig 22.3 The steady has been positioned about 5in (127mm) from the end of the goblet, and the outside profile is being fashioned with a spindle gouge. The tailstock is also providing additional support.

Fig 22.4 With the tailstock still giving support, much of the inside can be removed with the toe of a narrow skew chisel used scraper fashion.

photographs. While it is very easy to cut, it is extremely difficult to avoid breakages on the thin stem. I commend it to you, however, for practice purposes; it also smells nice, and is cheap!)

NATURAL-EDGE GOBLET
Yew wood is my favourite species for this type of goblet, the deeply contrasting colours of heart and sapwood very often producing spectacular effects. For the example, a limb about 8in (203mm) long is required.

Both pieces should be initially mounted between centres and a spigot cut at one end to suit your choice of chuck. In my case I formed a 2in (51mm) diameter spigot to fit the largest size O'Donnell jaws. A good, strong hold is required for this type of work or it will be extremely difficult to complete successfully.

STEADY
For any goblet over 9in (22.9cm), some kind of steady is essential. These can be home-made, and many books on woodturning include different types and methods of making.

ORDER OF WORK

LONG-STEMMED GOBLET
Fig. 22.2 shows the dimensional details for this goblet.

After securing the prepared piece in the chuck, bring up the tailstock for light support and carefully true up the cylinder with a roughing gouge. Excessive lathe speed is not necessary – 1400rpm is ideal.

Position the steady about 5in (127mm) from the cup end and apply candle wax to the revolving wood to minimize friction and noise. Set out the length of the cup and size in to about 1¼in (32mm) diameter. (Any smaller a diameter could create vibration problems even with a steady.) Commence shaping the outside profile with a ⅜in (10mm) spindle gouge, and clean up the end grain with the same tool (*see* Fig 22.3).

151

Fig 22.5 The tailstock has been removed to allow the inside of the cup to be completed with a gouge.

Some turners complete the hollowing first, but I am more concerned with the outside profile and so turn the inside to match.

Some of the inside can be removed with the skew chisel used scraper fashion and with the tailstock still providing support (*see* Fig 22.4).

With the tailstock removed the internal profile can be completed with a spindle gouge

and scraper (*see* Fig 22.5). Sand and polish the inside of the cup.

Pack the inside of the cup with kitchen paper and bring up the tailstock, applying light pressure only to help support the cutting of the thin stem (too much pressure will flex the stem).

Continue with the profiling at the base of the cup and determine the diameter of the stem where it merges with the cup. This will depend on your experience, skill and nerve. Cut back as close to the steady as you can and *gradually* taper the stem to get thicker. Fig 22.6 shows a spindle gouge being used for this purpose. Before repositioning the steady all of the profile completed to this stage must be sanded and polished. There is no coming back.

With the steady repositioned (and the lathe stationary), remember to back off the tailstock slightly before switching on. As a matter of habit I also spin the chuck with my hand before switching on to minimize the torque exerted on the stem and cup, otherwise it could well twist it off.

Continue with the removal of the bulk of the stem with a small roughing gouge, but a skew chisel is probably better for the final cuts. Fig 22.7 shows a skew being used like this, and cutting from right to left. I know that this is cutting against the grain, but I find it easier to arrive at the correct degree of taper this way,

Fig 22.6 The cup has been completed, sanded and polished. The inside has been packed with kitchen paper, allowing the tailstock to be brought up and provide extra support. A ¹⁄₄in (6mm) spindle gouge is being used to determine the thickness of the stem where it merges with the cup.

and light cuts with a sharp tool on a gentle uphill taper does no damage. Now sand and polish the stem you have just cut.

With the steady no longer required and moved out of the way, continue by removing the bulk of the waste with a small roughing gouge. Fig 22.8 shows the gouge in use, and the intended length of the goblet has been marked with a shallow cut with a parting tool. It may well be necessary to support the stem with the fingers of the left hand, as shown in the same photograph. Note the cutaway tool rest that enables me to hook my fingers behind the wood.

The curve on the base and the detail where the stem merges with it is perhaps best done with a ¼in (6mm) spindle gouge (see Fig 22.9). Now repeat the sanding and polishing process.

The goblet can now be parted off with a narrow parting tool (see Fig 22.10). Remember again to back off slightly with the tailstock support. Also remember that the encircling fingers of the left hand should only *cradle* the stem and *not grip* it. If you do you will probably break it, and at this late stage you would probably turn the air blue!

Finally, the base can be sanded on a disc sander or a Velcro-type abrasive gripped in a

Fig 22.7 The steady has been repositioned nearer the tailstock, enabling the next section of the stem to be cut. A small skew chisel is being used to cut the even taper. The fingers of the left hand are supporting the thin stem.

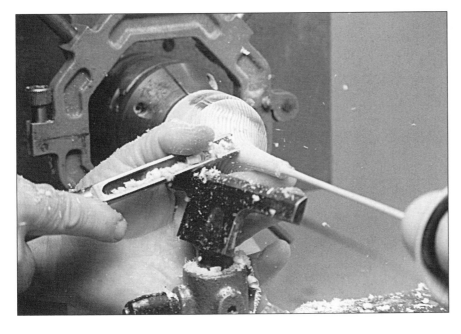

Fig 22.8 The steady has been removed and the bulk of the waste wood is seen being removed with a small roughing gouge (the fingers of the left hand again providing support).

153

Fig 22.9 The parting-off point has been established, and a ¼in (6mm) spindle gouge is being used to blend the base into the stem.

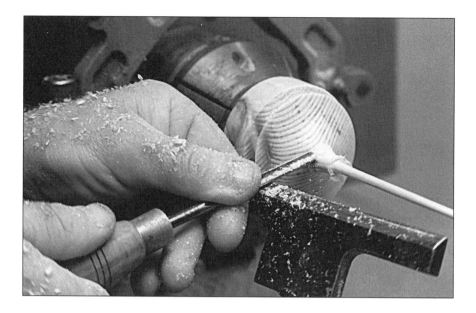

Jacobs chuck. It is quite possible to break the stem on this final operation if it is gripped too tightly. Hold it lightly and apply only gentle forward pressure against the sanding disc.

You can expect to break a few long, thin-stemmed goblets during your early attempts, but persevere and the rate of breakages reduces with experience – I promise!

NATURAL-EDGE GOBLET

Many of the steps described in the making of the long-stemmed goblet also apply to this. However, the mechanical steady is not used on this example. I am quite happy to rely on the

support of the tailstock (after hollowing out the inside of the cup) supplemented by my fingers.

Repeat the initial procedures used on the long-stemmed goblet to profile most of the outside of the cup and part of the inside, with the tailstock giving support. This must be removed to complete the gouging out of the inside, followed by sanding and polishing.

Repeat the packing of the cup with kitchen paper and bring up the tailstock for support. Reduce the first 2in (51mm) of the stem to about 1¼in (32mm) diameter.

The captive rings can now be formed, and the easiest way to do this is to make use of

Fig 22.10 Parting off with a ⅛in (3mm) parting tool. The tailstock has been backed off slightly, and the fingers are cradling the base and stem but *not gripping*. Gripping the stem tightly will break it.

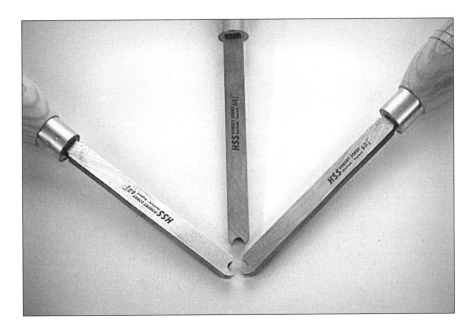

Fig 22.11 A set of Sorby Captive Ring Cutting tools.

Sorby Captive Ring Cutting tools. They come in various sizes, and each set comprises three different tools, each of which performs a separate function. Fig 22.11 shows the set used for the example, and Fig 22.12 (which is an adaptation of the Sorby instruction leaflet) provides a detailed explanation of their use (*see* page 162).

Fig 22.13 shows the right-hand tool starting the final cut to release the second ring.

The first stage of the 'anchor' now needs to be formed to the left of the captive rings. This is simply a saucer shape (the outside diameter should exceed the inside diameter of the rings), and Fig 22.14 shows a ¼in (6mm) spindle gouge being used to create the inside saucer shape and also to merge the tapered stem into it. Fig 22.15 is a view from the front, showing the outside profile of the 'saucer' and how the taper needs to be continued through it.

Fig 22.13 The first captive ring has been cut and the right-hand tool is being swung anticlockwise for the final cut on the second ring.

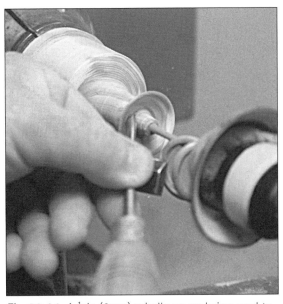

Fig 22.14 A ¼in (6mm) spindle gouge being used to form the internal saucer shape on the 'anchor'.

Fig 22.12 Instructions for using the captive ring tools.

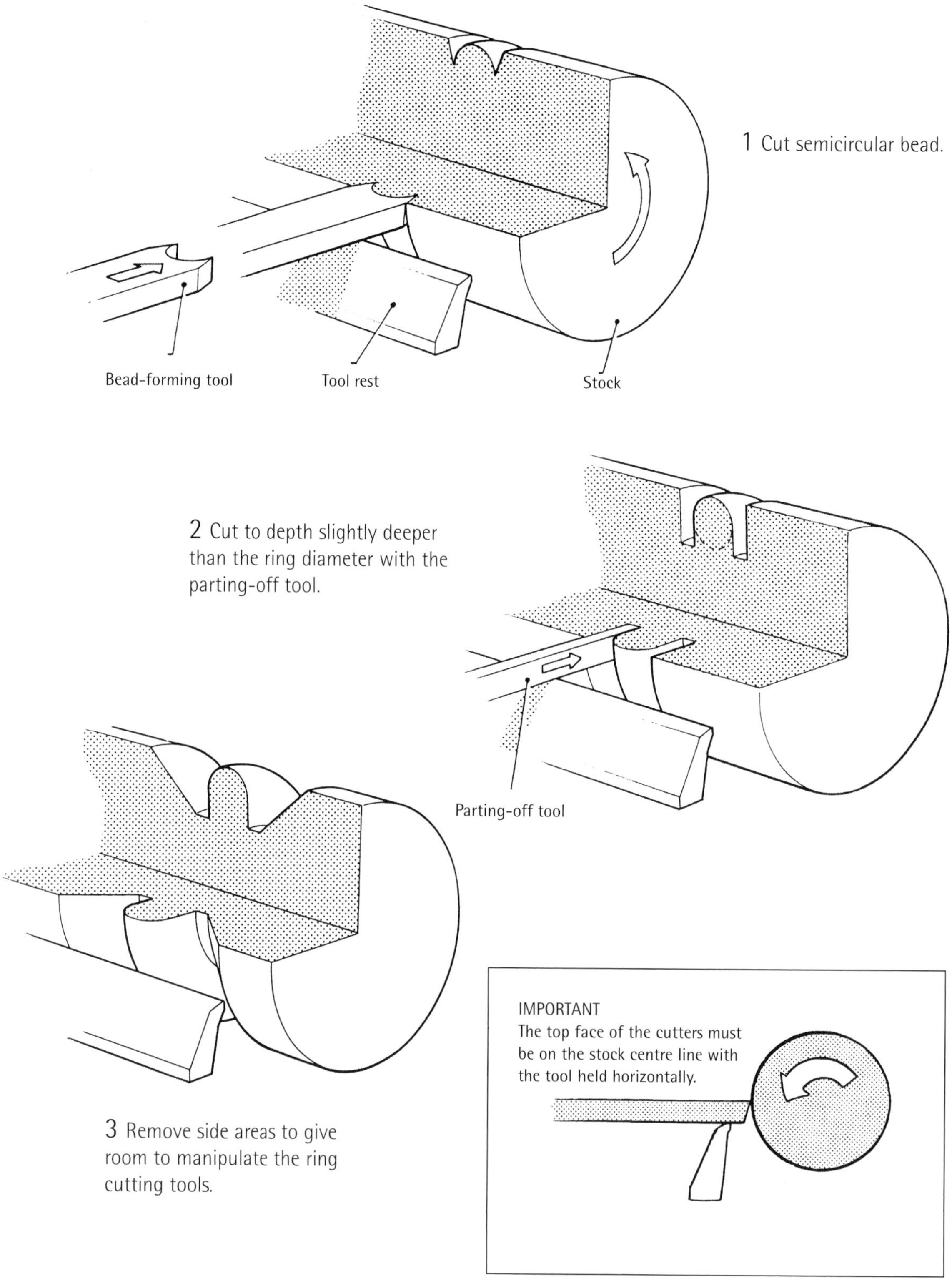

1 Cut semicircular bead.

Bead-forming tool   Tool rest   Stock

2 Cut to depth slightly deeper than the ring diameter with the parting-off tool.

Parting-off tool

3 Remove side areas to give room to manipulate the ring cutting tools.

IMPORTANT
The top face of the cutters must be on the stock centre line with the tool held horizontally.

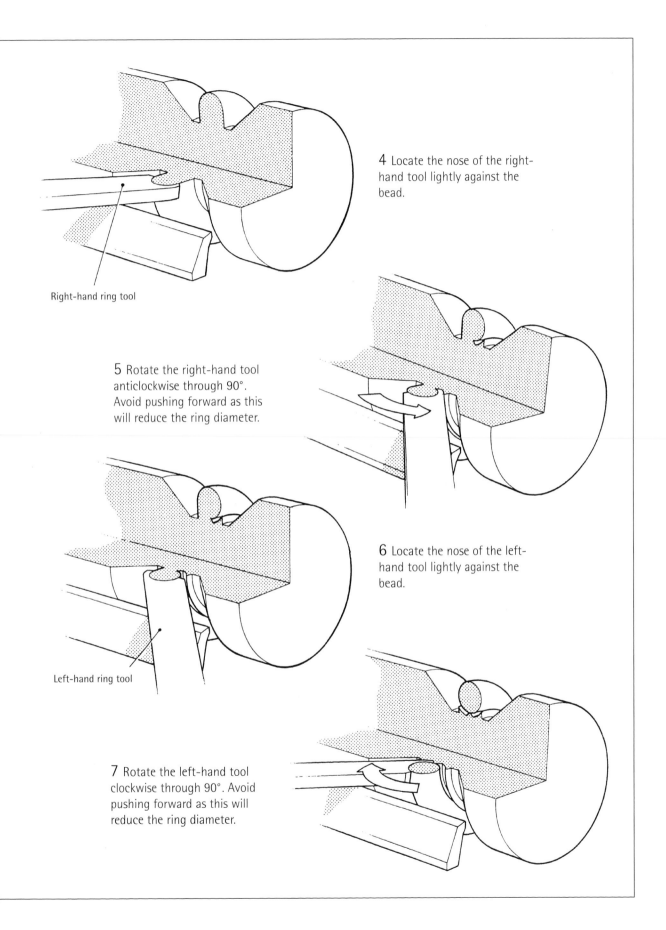

4 Locate the nose of the right-hand tool lightly against the bead.

Right-hand ring tool

5 Rotate the right-hand tool anticlockwise through 90°. Avoid pushing forward as this will reduce the ring diameter.

6 Locate the nose of the left-hand tool lightly against the bead.

Left-hand ring tool

7 Rotate the left-hand tool clockwise through 90°. Avoid pushing forward as this will reduce the ring diameter.

157

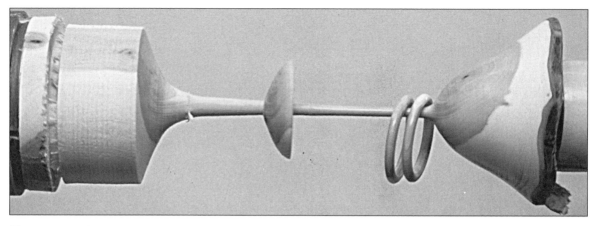

Fig 22.15 A view from the front of the lathe showing the outside profile of the 'anchor'. Note the gradual thickening of the stem from cup to base.

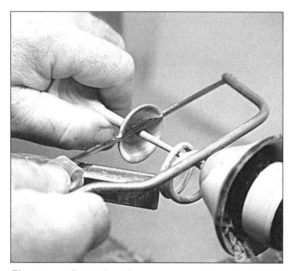

Fig 22.16 Removing the waste wood from the 'anchor' with a 'junior' hacksaw.

Making use of a 'junior' hacksaw, the bulk of the 'saucer' is then cut away. Great care must be taken to be gentle or the stem could fracture. Fig 22.16 shows the saw in use, and Fig 22.17 one side cut away.

This process is repeated on the other side of the 'saucer', and the remainder of the stem and base are profiled. As with the long-stemmed goblet, the sanding and polishing is done in stages as the work progresses. When using the fingers to steady the piece, great care must be taken to avoid them being injured by the whirling 'anchor'.

After parting off the underside can be sanded smooth and the 'anchor' shape can also be refined on the Velcro-type sanding disc, as shown in Fig 22.18.

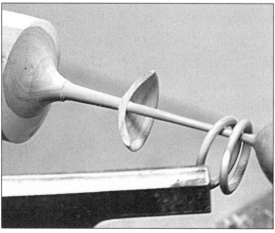

Fig 22.17 How the 'anchor' should look after the first cut.

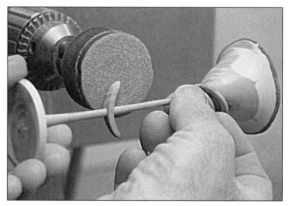

Fig 22.18 The profiling has been completed and the goblet has been parted off. A Velcro sanding system is being held in a Jacobs chuck and the shape of the 'anchor' is being refined.

FINISHING

Unless it is intended to spray-finish such pieces after completion, it is important to remember to sand and polish at each stage. I apply two coats of friction polish to all my goblets, and yew wood responds particularly well to it.

Goblets intended to be drunk from require special treatment, of course. Something like Rustin's Plastic Coating may be used, full instructions being supplied with the product (*see* page 162).

GENERAL COMMENTS

A vari-speed lathe is a great asset on this type of work. If any undue 'wobble factor' is encountered the speed can easily be adjusted until it disappears. When it is necessary to stop the lathe in order to adjust the lathe speed by the pulley system (or to reposition the steady), subsequent restarting can twist the stem from the cup.

To prevent this, always back the tailstock off very slightly and spin the chuck freehand while simultaneously pressing the start button. The tailstock can then be advanced to its original supporting position.

Having successfully completed both these difficult projects, make yourself one of the simpler and shorter-stemmed goblets shown in Fig 22.1. Fill it with wine and toast yourself. Cheers, and here's to more woodturning projects.

Safety in the Workshop

While the woodturning lathe is arguably the safest of all woodworking machines, there have been instances of serious injury being caused to the operator. In my opinion, the reasons for this can be put down to one of three things:

1 Ignorance of the correct techniques – incorrect methods are nearly always dangerous – and safety measures.

2 Taking unnecessary risks even when experienced. Most professional turners take 'acceptable' or 'calculated risks' to speed up production, but even so the chances of injury are increased, particularly when combined with number 3 below.

3 Tiredness or lack of concentration. The well-known saying 'familiarity breeds contempt' is particularly relevant to all wood machinists. It must be remembered that all machines can 'bite', and most accidents occur through lack of concentration and towards the end of the working day when tiredness has set in. My advice is to stop when you feel tired or if your mind is so engrossed on something else that it prevents you from applying maximum concentration.

The following list sums up basic rules for safe working practice.

SAFETY RULES

Ensure the electrics are safe – that is, the machine is properly earthed and installed in accordance with the maker's instructions. If a secondhand lathe is acquired, obtain the services of a qualified electrician to check it over. It will be money well spent.

- Rubber plugs should be fitted to all woodworking machines.
- Examine the electric cable from time to time to make sure it is in good order.
- Always isolate the lathe from the mains when changing speeds or applying the 'test of tightness'.

- Ensure that the lathe is securely bolted down to a good solid bench, in the case of a bench model, and occasionally check the tightness of the nuts.
- Sensible dress must be worn. Loose, dangling sleeves must be avoided at all costs. Good strong footwear is also very important. Tools are sometimes dropped or roll off the bench and can cause nasty wounds if you are shod in trainers or similar footwear.
- Use a purpose-built grindstone that is properly enclosed and designed to run at the correct speed. Occasionally check the soundness of the stone. Some form of eye protection must be worn when using the grindstone.
- Study the Laws of Woodturning, page 161. Breaking any one of them can be dangerous.
- Always examine the wood for faults, such as dead knots, splits, shakes, etc. If any of these are evident, discard the timber and find some sound stock.
- Ensure that all the locking handles have been tightened and the work spins freely before switching on the power.
- Always stand to one side and out of the 'firing line' when starting the machine.
- Make sure that there is no less than ¾in (19mm) of toolrest protruding by the end of the wood on which you are working.
- In the early learning stage, it is advisable to stop the lathe when making adjustments to the toolrest.
- Minimize the downward leverage on the tools by keeping the rest as close as possible to the workpiece.
- Always remove the toolrest when sanding. Wherever possible, sanding must be done in the 'safe' position.
- Some kind of protection against dust is essential. Make use of a dust mask and/or an extractor unit.
- Keep a fire extinguisher in the workshop and do not smoke or allow anyone else to smoke in the shop.

The above list is by no means exhaustive. Very often safety boils down to using your common sense, being patient and not taking risks.

A Summary of the Laws of Woodturning

Law 1 The speed of the lathe must be compatible with the size, weight and length of wood to be turned.

Law 2 The tool must be on the rest *before* the whirling timber is engaged, and must remain so whenever the tool is in contact with the wood.

Law 3 The bevel (grinding angle) of the cutting tools must rub the wood behind the cut.

Law 4 The only part of the tool that should be in contact with the wood is that part of the tool that is receiving *direct support* from the toolrest.

Law 5 Always cut 'downhill' or with the grain.

Law 6 Scrapers must be kept perfectly flat (in section) on the toolrest and presented in the 'trailing mode', i.e. with the tool handle higher than the tool edge.

NB: Experienced turners very often employ the 'shear scrape', where the scraper is tilted to approximately 45° and very often pointing upwards. This can be dangerous in unskilled hands.

Useful Addresses

Association of Woodturners of Great Britain,
SECRETARY: Peter Einig, Keeper's Cottage, Lee,
Ellesmere, Shropshire, SY12 9AE.

Axminster Power Tool Co.,
Chard St, Axminster, Devon EX13 5DZ.
Machinery, chucks, tools. Catalogue available.

John Boddy's Fine Wood and Tool Store,
Riverside Sawmills, Boroughbridge,
N. Yorks YO5 9LJ.
Machinery, chucks, wood and tools.
Catalogue available.

Carrol Sanders, 16–18 Factory Lane, Croydon,
Surrey CR0 3RL.
Quick-change sanding drums.

Bob Chapman Woodturning Accessories,
93 Parkway, Coxheath, Maidstone, Kent
ME17 4EX.
Light-pull drives, chuck accessories and specialist
tools. Catalogue available.

Peter Child, The Old Hyde, Little Yeldham,
Halstead, Essex CO9 4QT.
Instruction, wood, tools, chucks, lathes.
Catalogue available.

Craft Supplies Ltd, The Mill, Millers Dale,
Buxton, Derbyshire SK17 8SN.
Instruction, wood and all requirements.
Catalogue available.

Alan Holtham, The Old Stores, Wistaston Rd,
Willaston, Nantwich, Cheshire CW5 6QJ.
Instruction, wood and all requirements.

Christopher Milner Fine Woodcraft,
Beresford Lane, Woolley Moor, Nr Alfreton,
Derbyshire DE55 6FH.
Clocks, barometers, finishing material.

Myford Ltd, Chilwell Rd, Beeston, Nottingham
NG9 1ER.
Manufacturers of quality woodturning lathes and
accessories.

Bob Neil Pyrography, 10 Long Croft,
Aston-on-Trent, Derbyshire DE72 2UH.
Courses, demonstrations, equipment.

Robert Sorby Ltd, Athol Rd, Sheffield S8 0PA.
Lathes, chucks, turning and carving tools, specialist
tools and accessories.

Startrite Machine Tools Ltd, Norman Close,
Rochester, Kent ME2 2JU.
Bandsaws, pillar drills, planers, etc.

Chris Stott, Croft House, Burringham, South
Humberside.
Specialist hollowing tools; video: Natural Edges and
Hollow Forms.

Techlink Enterprises Ltd, 17 Hazel Way, Stoke
Poges, Slough SL2 4BW.
Precision fluting systems, router carriers,
indexing units.

Tyme Machines plc, Paragon House,
Flex Meadows, The Pinnacles, Harlow,
Essex CM19 5TJ.
Comprehensive range of lathes, bandsaws,
pillar drills and power tools.

Woodfit Ltd, Kem Mill, Whittle le Woods,
Chorley, Lancs PR6 7EA.
Scan fittings, cabinet and knock-down fittings.

SUPPLIERS OF WOOD-FINISHING PRODUCTS

Fiddes & Son, Florence Works, Brindley Rd,
Cardiff CF1 7TX.

Liberon Waxes Ltd, Mountfield Industrial Estate,
Learoyd Rd, New Romney, Kent TN28 8XU.

Rustins Ltd, Waterloo Rd, Cricklewood, London
NW2 7TX.

All three companies provide leaflets on their
products and advice on how to get the best from
them.

About the Author

Keith Rowley was born in Heanor, South Derbyshire. His interest in wood started early, when he left school to work in the National Coal Board's joinery section. The wide spectrum of skills he acquired included first fixing carpentry, cabinet making, wheel-wrighting and woodturning.

The demise of the coal industry in south Derbyshire in the late fifties prompted Keith to join the Nottingham City Police. He took early retirement from the Force in 1984 and has been woodturning on a professional basis ever since.

He balances his time now with a mixture of architectural turning, teaching, writing and demonstrating. Known to many woodturners through his demonstrations at the major woodworking exhibitions, Keith has also demonstrated at several international seminars and is much in demand at branches of the Association of Woodturners of Great Britain. He is a registered turner with the Worshipful Company of Turners and has been appointed as the organization's Official Assessor for the Midlands area. He is author of the highly popular book *Woodturning: A Foundation Course*.

METRIC CONVERSION TABLE

INCHES TO MILLIMETRES AND CENTIMETRES

mm = millimetres   cm = centimetres

INCHES	MM	CM	INCHES	CM	INCHES	CM
1/8	3	0.3	9	22.9	30	76.2
1/4	6	0.6	10	25.4	31	78.7
3/8	10	1.0	11	27.9	32	81.3
1/2	13	1.3	12	30.5	33	83.8
5/8	16	1.6	13	33.0	34	86.4
3/4	19	1.9	14	35.6	35	88.9
7/8	22	2.2	15	38.1	36	91.4
1	25	2.5	16	40.6	37	94.0
1 1/4	32	3.2	17	43.2	38	96.5
1 1/2	38	3.8	18	45.7	39	99.1
1 3/4	44	4.4	19	48.3	40	101.6
2	51	5.1	20	50.8	41	104.1
2 1/2	64	6.4	21	53.3	42	106.7
3	76	7.6	22	55.9	43	109.2
3 1/2	89	8.9	23	58.4	44	111.8
4	102	10.2	24	61.0	45	114.3
4 1/2	114	11.4	25	63.5	46	116.8
5	127	12.7	26	66.0	47	119.4
6	152	15.2	27	68.6	48	121.9
7	178	17.8	28	71.1	49	124.5
8	203	20.3	29	73.7	50	127.0

Index

GMC PUBLICATIONS

BOOKS

WOODTURNING

Adventures in Woodturning	*David Springett*	Practical Tips for Turners & Carvers	*GMC Publications*
Bert Marsh: Woodturner	*Bert Marsh*	Practical Tips for Woodturners	*GMC Publications*
Bill Jones' Notes from the Turning Shop	*Bill Jones*	Spindle Turning	*GMC Publications*
Carving on Turning	*Chris Pye*	Turning Miniatures in Wood	*John Sainsbury*
Colouring Techniques for Woodturners	*Jan Sanders*	Turning Wooden Toys	*Terry Lawrence*
Decorative Techniques for Woodturners	*Hilary Bowen*	Useful Woodturning Projects	*GMC Publications*
Faceplate Turning: Features, Projects, Practice	*GMC Publications*	Woodturning: A Foundation Course	*Keith Rowley*
Green Woodwork	*Mike Abbott*	Woodturning Jewellery	*Hilary Bowen*
Illustrated Woodturning Techniques	*John Hunnex*	Woodturning Masterclass	*Tony Boase*
Make Money from Woodturning	*Ann & Bob Phillips*	Woodturning: A Source Book of Shapes	*John Hunnex*
Multi-Centre Woodturning	*Ray Hopper*	Woodturning Techniques	*GMC Publications*
Pleasure & Profit from Woodturning	*Reg Sherwin*	Woodturning Wizardry	*David Springett*

WOODCARVING

The Art of the Woodcarver	*GMC Publications*	Wildfowl Carving Volume 1	*Jim Pearce*
Carving Birds & Beasts	*GMC Publications*	Wildfowl Carving Volume 2	*Jim Pearce*
Carving Realistic Birds	*David Tippey*	Woodcarving: A Complete Course	*Ron Butterfield*
Carving on Turning	*Chris Pye*	Woodcarving for Beginners: Projects, Techniques & Tools	
Decorative Woodcarving	*Jeremy Williams*		*GMC Publications*
Practical Tips for Turners & Carvers	*GMC Publications*	Woodcarving Tools, Materials & Equipment	*Chris Pye*

PLANS, PROJECTS, TOOLS & THE WORKSHOP

40 More Woodworking Plans & Projects	*GMC Publications*	Sharpening: The Complete Guide	*Jim Kingshott*
Electric Woodwork: Power Tool Woodworking	*Jeremy Broun*	Sharpening Pocket Reference Book	*Jim Kingshott*
The Incredible Router	*Jeremy Broun*	Woodworking Plans & Projects	*GMC Publications*
Making & Modifying Woodworking Tools	*Jim Kingshott*	The Workshop	*Jim Kingshott*

TOYS & MINIATURES

Designing & Making Wooden Toys	*Terry Kelly*	Making Wooden Toys & Games	*Jeff & Jennie Loader*
Heraldic Miniature Knights	*Peter Greenhill*	Miniature Needlepoint Carpets	*Janet Granger*
Making Board, Peg & Dice Games	*Jeff & Jennie Loader*	Restoring Rocking Horses	*Clive Green & Anthony Dew*
Making Little Boxes from Wood	*John Bennett*	Turning Miniatures in Wood	*John Sainsbury*
Making Unusual Miniatures	*Graham Spalding*	Turning Wooden Toys	*Terry Lawrence*

CREATIVE CRAFTS

The Complete Pyrography	*Stephen Poole*	Creating Knitwear Designs	*Pat Ashforth & Steve Plummer*
Cross Stitch on Colour	*Sheena Rogers*	Making Knitwear Fit	*Pat Ashforth & Steve Plummer*
Embroidery Tips & Hints	*Harold Hayes*	Miniature Needlepoint Carpets	*Janet Granger*
		Tatting Collage	*Lindsay Rogers*

UPHOLSTERY AND FURNITURE

Care & Repair	*GMC Publications*	Making Fine Furniture	*Tom Darby*
Complete Woodfinishing	*Ian Hosker*	Making Shaker Furniture	*Barry Jackson*
Furniture Projects	*Rod Wales*	Seat Weaving (Practical Crafts)	*Ricky Holdstock*
Furniture Restoration (Practical Crafts)	*Kevin Jan Bonner*	Upholsterer's Pocket Reference Book	*David James*
Furniture Restoration & Repair for Beginners	*Kevin Jan Bonner*	Upholstery: A Complete Course	*David James*
Green Woodwork	*Mike Abbott*	Upholstery: Techniques & Projects	*David James*
		Woodfinishing Handbook (Practical Crafts)	*Ian Hosker*

DOLLS' HOUSES & DOLLS' HOUSE FURNITURE

Architecture for Dolls' Houses	*Joyce Percival*	Making Period Dolls' House Accessories	*Andrea Barham*
The Complete Dolls' House Book	*Jean Nisbett*	Making Period Dolls' House Furniture	*Derek & Sheila Rowbottom*
Easy-to-Make Dolls' House Accessories	*Andrea Barham*	Making Tudor Dolls' Houses	*Derek Rowbottom*
Make Your Own Dolls' House Furniture	*Maurice Harper*	Making Victorian Dolls' House Furniture	*Patricia King*
Making Dolls' House Furniture	*Patricia King*	Miniature Needlepoint Carpets	*Janet Granger*
Making Georgian Dolls' Houses	*Derek Rowbottom*	The Secrets of the Dolls' House Makers	*Jean Nisbett*

OTHER BOOKS

Guide to Marketing	*GMC Publications*	Woodworkers' Career & Educational Source Book	*GMC Publications*

VIDEOS

Carving a Figure: The Female Form	*Ray Gonzalez*	Woodturning: A Foundation Course	*Keith Rowley*
The Traditional Upholstery Workshop		Elliptical Turning	*David Springett*
Part 1: *Drop-in & Pinstuffed Seats*	*David James*	Woodturning Wizardry	*David Springett*
The Traditional Upholstery Workshop		Turning Between Centres: The Basics	*Dennis White*
Part 2: *Stuffover Upholstery*	*David James*	Turning Bowls	*Dennis White*
Hollow Turning	*John Jordan*	Boxes, Goblets & Screw Threads	*Dennis White*
Bowl Turning	*John Jordan*	Novelties & Projects	*Dennis White*
Sharpening Turning & Carving Tools	*Jim Kingshott*	Classic Profiles	*Dennis White*
Sharpening the Professional Way	*Jim Kingshott*	Twists & Advanced Turning	*Dennis White*

MAGAZINES

WOODTURNING • WOODCARVING • BUSINESSMATTERS

The above represents a full list of all titles currently published or scheduled to be published. All are available direct from the Publishers or through bookshops, newsagents and specialist retailers. To place an order, or to obtain a complete catalogue, contact:

GMC Publications, 166 High Street, Lewes, East Sussex BN7 1XU United Kingdom
Tel: 01273 488005 Fax: 01273 478606

Orders by credit card are accepted